The Illustrated Guide to
Furniture Repair & Restoration

The Illustrated Guide to
Furniture Repair & Restoration

Edited by
Kitty Grime

ARCO PUBLISHING, INC. • Marshall Cavendish

New York   London & Sydney

Published by:

Marshall Cavendish Books
Limited
58 Old Compton Street
London W1V 5PA
England

IN THE U.K., COMMONWEALTH
AND REST OF THE WORLD,
EXCEPT THE UNITED STATES
OF AMERICA

Some of the material contained
in this book has already
appeared in other Marshall
Cavendish publications.

ISBN 0 85685 840 4

Arco Publishing, Inc.
219 Park Avenue South
New York, N.Y. 10003
U.S.A.

IN THE UNITED STATES OF
AMERICA

**Library of Congress Cataloging in
Publication Data**

Grime, Kitty.
 The illustrated guide to furniture
repair and restoration.

 1. Furniture finishing. 2 Furniture—
Repairing.
I. Title
TT199.4.G74 684.1'044 80-10795
ISBN 0-668-04936-7

Note: British spellings are used throughout this
book – the American equivalents appear in
square brackets after the British words, for
example: hessian [burlap] and calico [muslin].

Introduction

Choosing furniture is a very personal subject and no one piece will appeal to the same person. Trying to find the right sofa for the sitting room for example, can prove very difficult and also very expensive. One answer is to buy old or battered furniture – you can still find junk shop bargains – and restore and renovate them. But what you need to turn that unpromising buy into something everyone will be proud of, is patience and know-how. You provide the patience, this detailed book will provide the know-how.

Divided into easy-to-follow sections, you are advised what to look for when buying your furniture, how to salvage it and restore the glow and how to buy the right tools for the job. If you have no experience, it is best to acquire the basic skills of stripping, staining and varnishing and to start with simple repairs, for example mending a wobbly table leg. As you gain more confidence you can move on to more exciting projects such as veneering and repairing rush-type seating and cane furniture.

The full colour step-by-steps simplify the upholstery section which begins with renovating a drop-in dining chair seat with foam and builds up to restoring a chesterfield with traditional stuffing. The book can be used equally by a total beginner or a person who is perhaps already attending furniture repair classes and who wants to attempt more ambitious projects. All the skills detailed can be used on both old and modern furniture.

Whatever you attempt, the hours of hard work will be more than rewarded when your renovated piece of furniture is on display, admired by all, and totally unrecognizable from the unattractive article with which you started. You will also have discovered a hobby that, as well as being fun, is also worthwhile and creative.

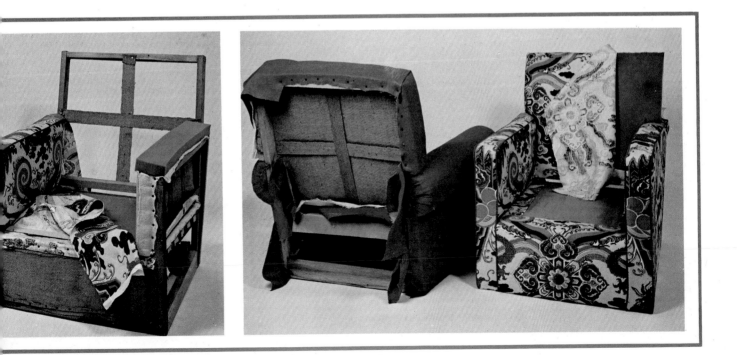

Contents

The Craft
of Buying
Old Furniture

Knowing what to look for when buying old or antique furniture is a skill that may take many years —and several mistakes—to acquire. There are even some who feel that recognizing a really fine old piece of furniture is an instinct which cannot be taught. Much wasted time, effort and cost can, however, be avoided by becoming acquainted with certain basic characteristics of good craftsmanship.

Nevertheless, it should be stressed that any hints regarding quality craftsmanship are not meant in any way to define the market value of a piece, but only constitute a guide to well-made furniture. This, then, will include reproduction furniture of all types, since many reproductions were made to the highest standards. Often, the only liability to a piece of reproduction furniture is that someone may try to pass it off as a genuine period piece.

What to look for

The furniture discussed below is quality-built (as opposed to mass-produced) and made prior to World War II. Any furniture made or fitted with the following materials is excluded.

1. All synthetics, i.e., poly-ethylene, nylon, plastic laminates, vinyl and acrylics.
2. All compressed particle board, i.e., chipboard, hard-board.
3. Plywoods—sheet materials made from laminated layers of veneers.
4. Blockboards—sheet materials made from lengths of wood glued together and faced on both sides with a thick veneer.
5. Nearly all the tropical woods, e.g., podo red or white marantti, iroko.
6. Japanese timber, e.g., Japanese oak, Japanese elm.
7. Pressed metal hinges and hardware fittings.
8. Plated and/or lacquered metal parts.
9. Rubber-shod castor wheels.

10. Wire nails or cross-head or Phillips screws.

In all furniture construction there is a major problem of wood movement—expansion on cold, damp days and contraction on warm days. This, together with the fact that wood is strongest in its length and weakest in its width, has dictated the methods of construction that must be used to make any piece of furniture properly. One of the more important things to look for, then, is that the wood grain of any components which are either adjacent or at right angles to each other, runs in one direction, otherwise the stresses created by shrinkage or expansion would cause the wood to split.

A typical cabinet
This could be either a chest of drawers, a bureau, a desk or a cupboard—any piece of furniture which was not mass-produced.

The most likely wood to be used would have been a hardwood, such as English, Yugoslavian or Austrian oak, French or English walnut, Spanish mahogany, sycamore, beech, birch, ash, chestnut or any other hardwood readily available to the local craftsman.

Top
A typical cabinet of almost any period would have the top and other large areas made out of several planks of solid wood in order to prevent bowing. These planks were planed along their longest edges until they were flat and square to the front of the cabinet. They were then placed together and rubbed one to the other until they mated perfectly. Finally, they were glued along these edges, or sometimes, if the boards were quite thick, they were held together with tongued-and-grooved joints.

Back
The backs, like the tops of cabinets, were susceptible to the same problems of bowing and timber movement, The traditional method of construction was to make the back with one or more panels, depending on the width, each with the grain pattern running vertically. Sides would be constructed in a similar manner. These panels were then joined together, where necessary, by vertical strips of wood about 75 mm (3 in) wide by 20 mm ($\frac{3}{4}$ in) thick, grooved on both edges. The panels were made to fit into these grooves without the use of glue. These back panels were fitted into grooves made in the wood of the sides, top and bottom of the piece. This construction method allowed the entire back to expand and contract without splitting. The best types of wood used were free from knots and planed smooth.

Sides
In good cabinet work the sides would have been made with a substantial front and back rail, or piece of wood, running vertically with an infill panel grooved and glued in between. Rails and side panels would be constructed in a hardwood of some kind and the wood grain, again, would run vertically. If top and bottom rails were used, the side panels would be constructed without glue to allow freedom of movement.

Left: *cast a knowing eye over these junk shop finds – all can be transformed.*

Fronts

The fronts of most cabinets usually consisted of rails running horizontally and vertically to form frames for the drawers and doors. It is important to note that they are securely fixed by mortise and tenon joints into the sides of the piece. In this joint, a tongue of wood is cut in one piece to fit exactly into a slot cut in the other. The two are held together with glue or dowels.

Drawers

The traditional construction of a drawer was the same, whatever its size. Drawer fronts would be made of hardwood, usually chosen to match the body of the cabinet, while sides, backs and bottoms could be made of any sound, stable wood. If plywood has been used the drawers are, of course, recently made. The sides should be held to fronts and backs with dovetail joints. Older dovetail joints were always hand-cut, and can be identified by the unequal size of the tails: machine-made dovetails are of equal size. The drawer bottom should slide in from the back into grooves cut in the sides and be fixed to the underside of the back. In a properly constructed drawer, the entire drawer should sit and slide on hardwood runners and should have side strips to stop it from tilting from side to side. One way of testing this is to try to open the drawer with one hand only. If well made, it should slide out smoothly, neither wobbling nor becoming wedged along one side.

Doors

The doors of a cabinet would be made of a hardwood frame with a grooved top, bottom and side rails to take a hardwood panel. To allow the wood to expand and contract, the panel would not be glued into the frame.

Finishes

In general, the quality of a finish is a good indication of the quality and value of the entire piece of furniture. On old furniture, the finishes most likely to have been applied are linseed oil for teak, oak, deal [Baltic pine] and beech, lime bleach and fuming for oak with a pale or medium tone, home-made beeswax and turpentine polish to give a protective finish, or a shellac dissolved in methylated spirits [denatured alcohol] finish for mahogany, walnut or more exotic hardwoods. The mirror-like surface achieved by the shellac and spirit [alcohol] finish, usually called French polishing, was the work of skilled craftsmen. The surface was made as flat and smooth as possible, then coat after coat of polish applied, each coat rubbed painstakingly down to the wood, to fill any minute crevices, until a final coat could be applied. The process brought out the depth and iridescence of the grain and it is usually easy to distinguish between a craftsman or a machine-applied finish. Old finishes were intended to protect and enhance the natural look of the wood, not to disguise it; heavy, sticky varnishes and thick

Left: *Great grandma's stately, old wardrobe gets today's mellow look when all those layers of varnish are removed.*
Opposite: *the right size, the right shape, the right price – all this plain piece needed was stripping and finishing.*

coatings of finish, are not found on good furniture. Painted finishes are easy to recognize; an old painted finish may make the piece more valuable, so before trying to restore or remove it get expert advice.

There are few finishes which cannot be restored, so do not bypass an attractive piece because the surface is in bad condition. When looking at an item, the quality of finish should be observed and especially the *patina* of the surface. This is a term used to refer to the surface that wood acquires after years of careful polishing and constant use, and it is one of the surest ways of distinguishing a genuinely old piece, as it cannot be faked. A surface with a good patina should have an almost translucent, mellow tone. It will be generally somewhat darker than the original wood colour (or lighter, if sunlight has bleached it). Beware of very shiny, perfectly polished pieces —this is recent work—and of pieces that have been darkly stained to hide an inferior grade of wood. If, as is likely, the grain has been filled with plaster [starch paste filler] and then heavily varnished, the surface will look muddy and opaque.

One further note: it is always possible for a cabinet maker to obtain some genuinely antique wood to make or restore a repro-duction piece—especially for sides or tops—but it is almost impossible to re-create a true patina. Once you have seen and touched the real thing, you will know what to look for.

Veneering
A veneer is a thin layer of wood, originally cut by hand, but cut by machine after the early nineteenth century. Exotic, richly-hued and beautifully figured woods have always been rare and highly prized. Veneering came into fashion in the eighteenth century and was used because it enabled craftsmen to use decorative but unstable and expensive woods in conjunction with inexpensive, stable but dull structural woods. The most precious kinds came into the hands of only the most skilful craftsmen.

They developed the art of matching veneers, taking adjacent sheets from the same log, to arrange them in symmetrical patterns to cover broad surfaces. The use of veneers also made possible such elaborate techniques as marquetry and inlay work. Beware of buying pieces of furniture where you can see that a veneered surface is beginning to rise or warp. Many can be repaired but it would be wise to have the condition appraised by an expert before you spend much money.

Mouldings and decorations
On the best furniture, mouldings

and decorations are carved into the solid rails or panels. However, if they are applied, they should be jointed and glued in—*not* simply held in place by fine nails or pins. Do not think that a piece must be authentic because it is inlaid. This was often done to make it look more ornate and to raise its price.

Hinges and hardware fittings
The very best hardware fittings and hinges were made in brass or bronze, either cast or hand-cut from a plate and soldered with silver. Naturally, on really old

pieces, these will be somewhat dull and scratched from wear. Also, there will be a noticeable difference in the colour of the wood beneath these fittings, and most likely there will be rust marks on the wood.

Other distinguishing features

There will be some differences in construction because of the tools, nails and screws used in old furniture. Before the eighteenth century, for instance, wood was cut with straight saws. In the nineteenth century, circular saws were introduced which cut the wood faster and left ridges around the cut which can be felt with the finger. Generally, nails and screws are not a good guide to the quality or genuineness of a piece as they are easy to fake. Up to 1790 nails were hand-cut, and thereafter machine-pressed. Wooden screws were first made over 300 years ago. They had no taper (until the nineteenth century) and the slots on top were usually off-centre. The threads were hand-filed with a shallow spiral in them. One thing you might look for when appraising a piece with nails is an oxidizing stain on the wood. This obviously is a sign of age.

Of course, there are many fine pieces of furniture which have been made at a later date and which do not conform to these traditional methods of construction, but in any pieces which you suspect to be quite old, check the points mentioned for quality and authenticity. Genuineness is a problem in itself. It may, however, not be important. If a piece is well-made, performs its functions and is good value for money, why not consider buying a reproduction?

In any case, there are few absolutes in judging quality in old and antique furniture. The number of people who can spot a fake is surprisingly small. Check against the guidelines mentioned if you are making an investment in a good quality piece. The safest thing you can do, after you have investigated the piece as best you can, is to get a written description from the seller. If it proves to be completely false, you have a good case for returning the piece and getting your money back.

If the piece is in doubtful condition, never mind the dirt or the broken legs but avoid loose joints in any quantity, panels with broad cracks in them, or tide-marked wood which shows exposure to damp. Above all, keep a sharp look-out for signs of attack by fungi and woodworm. Train your nose to differentiate between the dusty and the musty. Avoid pieces with clumsy repairs that destroy the original character of the piece: screws visibly placed, nailed patches, metal rods or wires. Most broken legs can be repaired, the simpler ones even replaced. But if you come across an elaborately curved leg with a compound fracture, involving splits down the grain and loss of timber, remember that you will not be able to mend or replace it yourself unless your skills resemble those of the original maker.

Left: *if you are furnishing on a budget, these typically non-precious pieces can be just what you are looking for. Carefully restored they can add a touch of class to your home.*

Wood Selection and Furniture Salvage

Wood Selection

Most of the old and antique furniture you will come across will be made almost entirely of wood which was freely available to craftsmen in earlier times. To make the best possible assessment of secondhand pieces, the more you know about wood the better. As species and sub-species run literally into thousands, you would need to be an expert indeed to name different woods on sight. However, in the secondhand furniture market, you have a relatively small selection to familiarize yourself with. If starting from scratch, look at a set of education samples or get a book from your library and study the grains, which are a surer guide than colour (often disguised by skilful varnishing). Look at museum pieces if you can. This will give you some idea of the typical woods used for each period and kind of furniture. Try not to mistake the finish for the wood.

Hardwoods

Hardwoods and semi-hardwoods come from deciduous trees and include ash, beech, birch, cherry, elm, gum, mahogany, maple, oak, poplar, rosewood, satinwood, sycamore, teak and walnut.

The majority of hardwood supplies come from tropical countries; Africa (particularly West Africa), Burma, Sri Lanka, India, Japan, Thailand and the West Indies. Some important hardwoods grow also in Australia, and Central, North and South America are becoming important sources of supply as the world's timber resources dwindle. Hardwoods are durable, densely textured and give surfaces which are easy to smooth and polish to a fine finish. The

mature hardwood used for furniture-making is the heartwood. Cabinet makers were skilled in picking the right wood for the job, from their knowledge of each kind's performance and specific peculiarities.

Ash
A European wood which is coloured creamy white with a grain similar to oak. It is tough and very hard, but also bends well and is often used for the bowed backs of Windsor chairs. It is traditionally used for tool handles because of its durability.

Beech and birch
Both are hard, dense woods, with very little obvious grain figure. Beech is a plentiful native British wood and was therefore used for everyday items such as bench tops, carpentry tools, butchers' blocks, chopping and bread boards (the wood will not taint the taste of food), as well as common household furniture, particularly chairs. The surfaces are smooth and sheer with little grain indentation and they can take a fine polish. Beech varies in tone from brownish pink to yellowish white; birch is usually whitish.

Cherry
This is a fairly light, but solid timber with a lively, close grain with tiny rays that reflect the light and a golden sheen. It is used in craftsman-made furniture, and today in decoratively turned woodware like fruit bowls and ornamental boxes.

Elm
This wood was traditionally used for rough furniture, farm implements and coffins, as it was thought too unstable and difficult to work for fine furniture. Following the enormous loss of elms through Dutch elm disease, elm is now more widely available, as the disease attacks the bark, not the actual wood. Modern furniture-making methods have 'tamed' elm; it is tough, attractive, responds well to wood stains and polishes and is used for a wide range of furnishings. English elm is light to reddish brown, open and coarse-grained, with considerable grain variation which adds to the interesting look of the wood.

Mahogany
Antique mahogany has the rich, dark reddish colour which most people associate with this type of wood. In previous centuries, this naturally exotic colour was also emphasized by dark stains and surface treatments. Modern mahogany is much lighter in colour, not so hard, and does not often have the same markedly wild and decorative grain patterning. Leave mahogany in the sun and it may bleach to a golden yellow. The darker kinds come from West Africa and the lighter, pinkish ones from Central America and Guyana. Sapele is a species of mahogany: with its unique striped grain it is used as a veneer on modern furniture.

Oak
English oak is probably the strongest, most dense oak there is, but the only reasonably priced source nowadays is through the reclaim market—from old furniture, buildings and boats, for example. Oak is notable for being resistant to woodworm and rot, which is why a lot of very good antique oak furniture has survived the centuries. With age it can become almost black-brown—reproduction furniture gets this look by staining. Oak is hard to work, but the cut surfaces have clean, sharp edges. It has an open-grain texture, often filled with grain filler before the finishing treatment. The acid in oak discolours and rusts steel or iron screws and fittings. Use zinc-plated screws or, traditionally, insert a steel screw, then remove and replace with a brass one.

Rosewood
This has always been rare and prized

Here are specimens of typical hardwoods used in furniture.
The top half of each piece shows the colour of the raw wood; the lower part how it looks after finishing.

Top left to right:
African walnut
Afrormosia
European ash
European beech
European elm
Iroko

Bottom left to right:
Rio rosewood
Sapele
Satinwood
Sweet chestnut
Sycamore
Burma teak

for its exotic colour and grain. Two major types are East Indian (a dark, purplish brown) and Brazilian or 'Rio' rosewood (a rich brown heartwood with an exotically wild grain). Both types are found mainly as veneers.

Satinwood

A light coloured, sometimes even lemon coloured, wood with rich figuring, often imitated on other woods by craftsmen making reproduction furniture. The wood takes a fine finish and is often highly polished.

Sycamore

A strong, pale, whitish wood which has distinct rays and rings and a mixture of straight and wavy grain which produces an attractive rippled effect. It is used for veneers, table tops and cabinets, as well as for decorative wall panels.

Teak, afrormosia, iroko

These are not traditional antique furniture woods. However, solid Burma, Siam and Indian teaks are becoming rare and expensive, so good quality modern teak furniture is probably the antique of the future. Today veneered and 'teak type' furniture is the most usual. The real thing is one of the hardest, heaviest, densest woods known, and needs no upkeep other than an occasional rub with teak oil.

Walnut

This is a high quality wood, relatively easy to carve and work and used traditionally for fine furniture. It is usually lightish brown in colour with distinctive brown to black markings.

Hardwoods respond well to a brisk polish with a little furniture cream or wax polish. Do not overdo the polish; too much builds up a sticky surface which traps dirt. Remember that you are protecting, not 'feeding' the wood. Wiping with a cloth barely dampened in soapy water does no harm, if the surface is thoroughly dried before it is polished.

Softwoods

Softwoods come from coniferous or evergreen trees, often classed under the broad heading of 'pines'. As they grow more quickly than hardwoods and can flourish in cooler climates, they tend to be cheaper and more plentiful. They include cedar, cypress, Douglas fir, hemlock, larch, pine, redwood, spruce and yew. The greatest reserves of softwood are in Canada and other parts of North America, and in Russia.

It is hard to distinguish between varieties of softwood because there is far less variety in colour and grain pattern than there is in hardwoods. Consequently, much softwood is simply called 'deal', although there is no such thing as a deal tree. Other names are redwood [red pine] and whitewood [white fir or white deal], describing the colour of the wood rather than referring to the name of the tree from which it was cut.

Softwoods are used for every part of house construction and decoration. (Spruce in America is very hard, difficult to work and tends to shrink, and yew [European or American] is a rare and hard-to-work wood, used mainly as a veneer.) They have always been used for furniture in the less elegant parts of the house, for nurseries, back bedrooms, kitchens and storage pieces. Because the wood was regarded as inexpensive, common and not particularly pretty, pieces were frequently painted. Today, the vogue is to buy up an old painted piece, strip it back to the wood and then protect the surface with a transparent sealer coat to keep the natural look. Coloured wood stains are also used to tint the surface without masking the grain pattern. Some kind of sealer coat must be applied or softwoods discolour and look dirty very quickly.

Left: *yesterday this plain pine chest lived in a back bedroom. Now, stripped of its paint it can go anywhere.*

Furniture Salvage

You will, of course, leave a precious, old, or particularly beautiful piece of furniture alone—and take professional advice on its restoration. But there are bargains in secondhand furniture to be found, which, if awkward and unattractive as they stand, can be separated into smaller, more useful units, and re-finished to give years of new life.

Suitable items

Look for pieces like the very ordinary dressing table in the picture which was separated into several useful items, and then for chests of drawers, old sideboards, wardrobes and dressers. The construction must be sound and the structure intact. Inspect the possibilities of a likely-looking piece. Check that the wood is solid; this makes re-finishing, cutting and re-assembling easier. Inspect the carcass—that is, the inside construction or frame which holds the outer surfaces together. The outside surfaces are often only panels and not part of the load-bearing structure. See how the frame is put together and where cuts can conveniently be made. Note how the dressing table was divided up; the top two drawers are complete with an additional bottom piece, a new top was added to the bottom drawer to make a telephone seat.

Once you have decided where to separate the unit—but before you make any cuts—it is wise to work out just what you intend to use to replace the supports that some horizontal components may be giving to

Right: there is nothing special about this dressing table as it stands. But what you can turn it into is quite another story.

two segments in the original unit, but can only give to one of them when they have been separated. The best solution is often a sheet of blockboard or chipboard, veneered or plain, according to its position. Generally, it is a good idea to work from the top, cutting immediately under horizontal components. If you have to replace a frame component adjoining a panel, remember that panels are never glued into their grooves, but left free to shrink as all wood does across the grain with time.

Cutting the unit

Unless you are going to cover the outside completely with paint, laminate or some other finish, try to avoid cracks and splintering as you saw. Any damage to the exterior surfaces will have to be put right.

Work into the panels from each edge, rather than sawing straight through. Draw a trimming knife along the cutting lines to sever the surface fibres before sawing. Since you intend to use both sections when separated, make the cutting lines double—say 3 mm ($\frac{1}{8}$ in) apart and saw between them. Before cutting make sure that there are no screws or nails along the cutting lines. You may need to devise some means of holding one section together while sawing through its

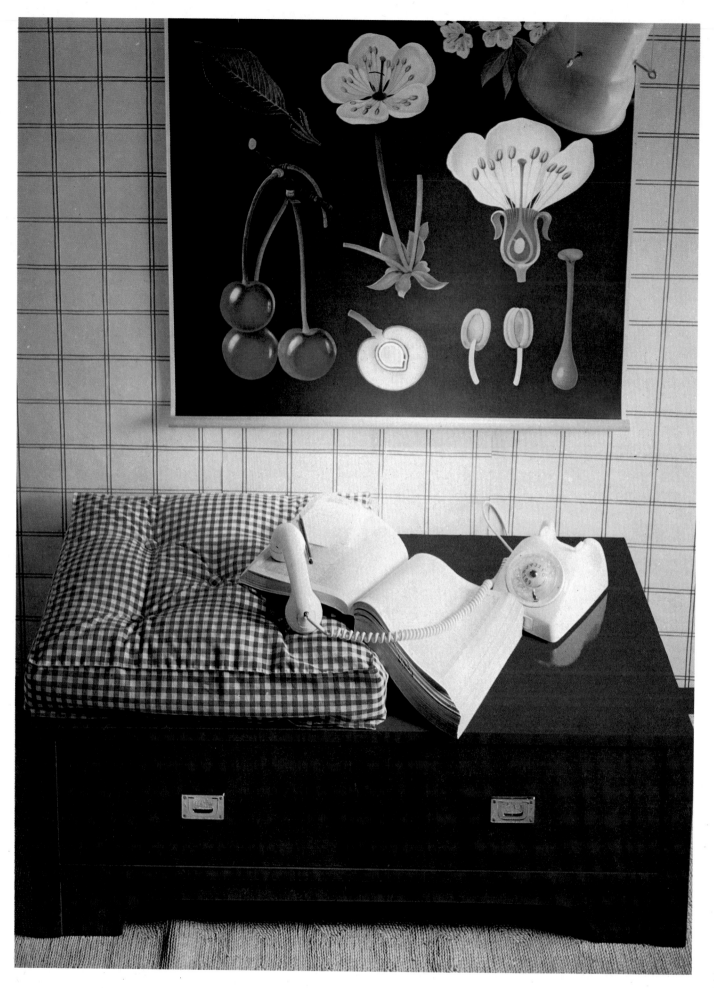

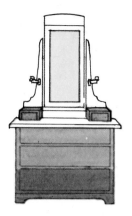

This dressing table was divided to make five useful pieces.

The mirror was unscrewed, the curved top piece cut off, so that it could be used as a decorative piece.

These candlesticks can be unscrewed from the dressing table, affixed to blocks of wood, and attached to a wall.

Below right: *the two small drawers from the dressing table top were unscrewed, cleaned up and glued together to make a neat little desk unit.*

Below left: *the two upper drawers of the dressing table were turned into a smart military-style chest with a coat of shiny black paint and brass trim, hardware and castors.*

Opposite: *after cutting, a top and handles were added to the bottom section of the dressing table to make a telephone seat.*

supporting components if the piece is delicate.

Use a sharp, fine-toothed, straight-bladed saw, such as a handsaw and make sure the blade has enough depth for the work. Saw cuts can be trimmed with a sharp, finely-set plane. The knife guide lines, if accurate, will prove invaluable in planing down to a really clean, straight line—essential if you want a really neat join with a new base or top.

Securing a new base or top

There are several methods for attaching new surfaces. You can, for example, screw from the top into the severed frame components. If you do screw down a new top, use a screw-sink [counter] bit to make the guide or pilot holes. These leave a neat recess over the sunken screwhead which can be filled with a plug of wood filler. Since the new units are not likely to be the same size as any standard veneered chipboard or blockboard panel, you will have to re-edge the board for a neat look. You can buy a matching pre-glued flexible edging strip which is easy to fix to a clean square edge, following manufacturer's instructions. Wood strips or beading [molding] can be nailed, screwed or glued to hide raw

edges. Use adhesive or glue where possible, as screws or nails will have to be sunk and filled for a neat look. Use edging clamps to hold the wood strips or fillets while the glue sets, or improvise a tourniquet from a pair of old tights or panty hose, tightened around the board and edging strip.

Hardware

Castors may make a piece more useful and moveable, but be sure to buy a set to match the total weight of the unit plus contents. Weaker ones will tend to collapse. Castors are only as strong as their fixings, so make sure that attaching screws are long enough to anchor them firmly into a solid section of wood. If necessary, screw and glue thick corner pieces on the underside of the unit and mount the castors on them. New hardware may need to be added or replaced. Unless it is of the simple lay-on kind, which can be screwed directly to the surface, a new recess may have to be cut. Draw carefully around the piece of hardware exactly where you want it. Use a hard, sharp pencil or angled knife point or scriber. Cut into the wood with a chisel, following the outline, then gently chip away the waste to the same depth.

Tools
and Their
Uses

Here are suggestions for a basic tool kit to see you through most of the furniture repair jobs in this book. If you have to buy any tools, consider each one an investment, as it is bound to be in regular use for repair jobs in your home. Borrow or rent anything special, like a power tool and attachments. You will need some specialist tools for upholstery, re-seating, veneering and furniture finishing; there are details of these in the appropriate chapters.

Holding

A vice [vise] is the basic holding tool to keep materials firm while you cut or work on them. A portable vice [vise]—at least a 25 cm (10 in) woodworking vice [vise] is necessary—can be clamped on any firm surface. If you have no workbench, use the kitchen table. Clamps are also useful to hold work to a firm surface or hold repairs together when gluing. Make a 'bench hook' to protect your work surface when cutting small pieces of wood. You need a ply or chipboard scrap 15 cm (6 in) by 30 cm (12 in) with two softwood stop strips, each 50 × 25 mm (2 × 1 in), one glued in one corner of the larger piece, the other in the opposite corner underneath the larger piece. Clamp the bench hook to your work surface.

Measuring and marking

A steel tape rule for general measurements. A 70 cm (2 ft) four-fold folding rule. A 30 cm (12 in) steel rule, also for use as a straight edge. A trimming knife for marking the wood (this is more accurate than a pencil). A try [or combination] square for checking and marking right angles. A marking or mitre gauge for marking lines parallel to an edge.

Cutting

A good average crosscut hand saw is a 55 cm (22 in) long, 10-point one for cutting large pieces of timber across the grain (ripsaws are for

Right: *treat your special tools with care, by using a mallet gently to avoid splitting the wood handles.*

cutting with the grain—a 5½-point is ideal). A tenon or back saw is used for finer work. This has a stiffened back piece to ensure a straight cut. A coping saw for cutting irregular shapes. A handyman's knife with assortment of blades.

Shaping and smoothing

A medium smoothing plane about 25 cm (10 in) long takes care of planing wood on the bench, edges and surfaces. For planing edges in cabinet work you need a low-angle block plane—about 18 cm (7 in) long. Chisels are used for basic shaping, joint cutting, chipping out small areas of unwanted wood. A firm chisel is used for basic work, a bevel-edged chisel for finer work. A set of three, 25 mm (1 in), 13 mm (½ in) and 6 mm (¼ in) will take care of most jobs.

Drilling

A hand drill plus a variety of woodworking bits is useful, but a push drill with spiral drive is invaluable for light cabinet work. A gimlet or bradawl is useful for starting screw holes.

Joining
Hammers

The right tool for the job makes all the difference. To most people a hammer is simply a tool to drive a nail home. However, different hammers vary in their function and each type is available in various weights. Some of the more common hammers have a specific function.

Claw hammer: 200 – 850 g (7 – 30 oz), is used for general purpose carpentry, particularly for driving and removing nails. When removing nails make sure that the nail is well into the claw, then lever evenly.

Warrington or cross pein [peen] hammer: 170 – 450 g (6 – 16 oz), is used for general nailing, joinery and metal beating.

Ball pein [peen] or engineer's hammer: 110 g – 1.4 kg (4 oz – 3 lb), is used for metal working. The round end is for starting rivets; its face is hardened steel and will not chip.

Pin or telephone [tack] hammer: 100 – 110 g (3½ – 4 oz), is used for tacks, panel pins [finishing nails] and fine nailing. The wedge-shaped end is used for starting small nails while holding them between the fingers.

Mallets

There are two basic types of mallet—

Carpentry mallet: used in carpentry and cabinet making.

Carver's mallet: used for creative woodwork.

Screwdrivers

Standard slotted screwdriver: this is used for general driving of single slotted screws.

Spiral ratchet screwdriver: this is used for general purpose screwdriving. By pushing in the handle it automatically drives or removes screws. When locked, the ratchet allows the screw to be driven or removed without taking it from the

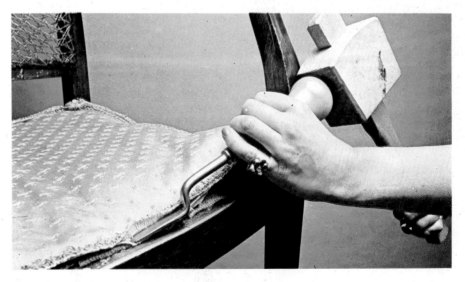

screw slot. Screw bits of different sizes can be fitted into the chuck, making this a very versatile tool.

Crosshead or Phillips screwdriver: this is used with modern cross-slotted screws to provide greater grip between the tip and the screwhead.

Tools and their maintenance

The simplest way of dealing with the problem of tool maintenance is to make sure that you keep the need for it to the minimum. Store tools properly, use them for their intended purpose only and do not drop them or knock them about. However, even with the most careful and knowledgeable treatment, most kinds of tools need a little attention from time to time to keep them at their most efficient. Apart from abuse, they have two other main enemies.

Rust

Good storage conditions are essential to keep rust at bay. Even in a 'dry' place, condensation can occur when the weather is cold unless the tools are in close proximity to rust-inhibiting paper, or coated with oil or lacquer. Linseed oil is suitable for coating tools (not as a lubricant). Apply it with a wad of cotton wool or absorbent cotton. If rust has appeared on a tool, steel wool and fine oil will remove it without much trouble. Rust that is too heavy or thick for this treatment may well have ruined the tool.

Wear

Most good tools should last a lifetime or more, and many improve with age. What wears out many tools is not hard work but sheer lack of lubrication. Tools do not need much oil—quite the contrary—but they do need the right kind and in the right places.

Lubricants

Little and often is a good rule. If a tool is used every day or once a week, its working parts could do with a drop or two: once a month is a good idea anyway, whether the tool is in use or not, because the fine oil used contains a high pro-

portion of paraffin and tends to dry out to some extent. To choose a suitable oil for your tools, read the contents label on the can and avoid those containing molybdenum or graphite. If in doubt, ask your hardware dealer for advice.

Super-duty lubricants: the idea of using a super-duty lubricant at infrequent intervals is very tempting, and can work out very well in some instances, but there are certain limitations. Oils and grease containing extreme pressure (EP) [HP] lubricants like molybdenum disulphide or graphite should be avoided because their molecules do not break down easily under pressures lighter than those for which they are designed, such as in a car engine. Pressures such as these are never encountered in hand-tool applications. This means that their super-tough particles remain as a

fine abrasive which can create rapid wear.

Grease: all greases have one disadvantage—they tend to pick up dust and grit. So they are best used only in enclosed situations, such as a hand drill with enclosed gear casing. If you must use grease, choose a general-purpose, light silicone one. Hand drills and bit and braces need only light oiling of the moving parts, including the brace head mountings and chuck threads. There is no need to dismantle the tool; a drop of oil in the places indicated will work its way into the tool. Power tools should have the lead cable and motor professionally examined after every 50 hours of use. This may mean having the tool serviced every six months or every two years, according to the amount of use it gets. A power tool should not be allowed to work without

regular servicing, just because it is going well. Do not oil or grease a power tool; if you do, misplaced oil can do more harm than good. With regular servicing there is no need for further lubrication.

A metal tape rule or measure should not need lubrication unless it has become accidentally wet, in which event the rule should be fully extended and wiped dry. Return the rule to its case, then extend again and wipe with a lightly oiled rag as the rule slips back. This may help to prolong its life if the water has seeped into the internal works.

Benches and clamps

Your work bench is a tool, a gripping device and a reference for edge and surface flatness. If a bench is used with care, the occasional wiping over with a finely-set low-angle plane should be all it needs, apart from oiling or lacquering to protect the wood. A very rough or uneven top may be better covered with a new, thick section board: chipboard is especially suitable, being flat and relatively inexpensive.

If a vice [vise] jams or rocks about, it can be more of a hindrance than a help to you, if not a positive danger. So tighten structural bolts or screws from time to time. Partially dismount the vice [vise] to clean and oil it.

Replace wooden jaw linings of a vice [vise] before they are so worn as to mark your wood, using a hardwood such as beech. Cut the new lining to the same size as the one you remove and screw or bolt it back in place.

G [C]-clamps: a little oil on the thread and in the small ball-joint at the screw-end foot should keep a G [C]-clamp working efficiently. These clamps are made from malleable iron, so if you drop one and knock it out of line, it is possible to hammer it back straight again, with care.

Striking tools

Screwdrivers, hammers and mallets are subject to the worst abuse. Hammers need frequent checking to ensure the snug fit of handle to head. This is because of the way they are used, not because they are shoddily made—assuming that you have bought a reputable brand, which is always advisable.

Once a head is loose, do not be tempted to soak the tool in a bucket of water. This only swells the fibres in the hammer 'eye' and destroys their strength. Have the handle replaced or, if the head is worn as well, buy a new one before it does

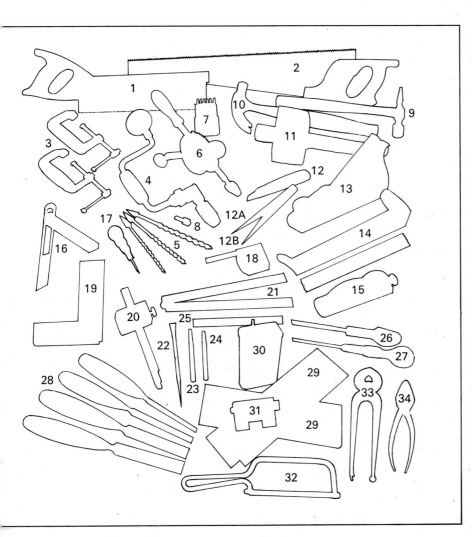

1. *Tenon or back saw*
2. *Handsaw*
3. *G [C] clamps*
4. *Ratchet brace*
5. *Wood auger bits*
6. *Hand drill*
7. *Twist bits*
8. *Countersink bit*
9. *Warrington or cross pein (peen) hammer*
10. *Claw hammer*
11. *Carpenter's or Joiner's mallet*
12. *Handyman's knife*
13. *Bench plane*
14. *Surform plane*
15. *Block plane*
16. *Sliding bevel*
17. *Bradawl or scratch awl*
18. *Adjustable steel rule*
19. *Carpenter's or try square*
20. *Marking gauge*
21. *Folding boxwood or wooden rule*
22. *Scriber marking knife*
23. *Nail punch [punch or nail set]*
24. *Centre punch for metal*
25. *Carpenter's pencil*
26. *Crosshead or Phillips screwdriver*
27. *Cabinet screwdriver*
28. *Carpenter's chisels*
29. *Oilstones*
30. *Fine machine oil*
31. *Honing gauge*
32. *Junior or small hacksaw*
33. *Pincers*
34. *Slipjoint pliers.*

someone harm. Inspect the striking face frequently. Any sign of cracks or chipping on the head indicates the need for a replacement. A chip flying from a faulty hammer face can reach the velocity of a bullet and do much damage. Clean the striking surfaces with sandpaper so that any damage is easily seen. Cracks in wooden handles can also be dangerous if not mended when they first appear.

Mallets are made from hardwood, usually beech, so a drop of linseed oil now and then stops them drying out. They may need occasional re-facing with a finely set sharp plane, but with correct use on materials softer than their own wood, this is rarely necessary. A loose head can be cured by tapping the tool upside down on a firm surface.

Brushes

Brushes are often neglected. They rarely get attention until so clogged up with dried paint or varnish that major doses of paint stripper are needed to clean them—and then it is often too late. To keep a good paintbrush in working condition, clean it scrupulously in the appropriate solvent immediately after use, then wash in warm water and detergent. Dry the brush, smoothing the bristles into shape and store in a plastic bag, which can be secured around the handle with a rubber band. Store flat or hanging. If brushes are in regular use, you might suspend them constantly in a tin of brush cleaner, filled to the top of the bristles and re-filled as the solution evaporates. If you let the brush rest on its bristles, you will deform the shape.

Chisels

Although a chisel is probably the most efficient cutting tool in existence, it is also the most dangerous. Careful storage is essential, and correct sharpening necessary to keep the cutting edge efficient. You will need the right carborundum oil stone and a few drops of oil. Hold the chisel with the bevel side flat on the stone at an angle of about 30°. Work back and forth, varying the tool's position on the stone to save wear. Turn the chisel over and draw the back edge across the stone to remove any burrs.

Screwdriving tools

The two main types are hand screwdrivers and spiral-ratchet screwdrivers. Each type includes screwdrivers of various sizes or bits to cope with the slots in the heads of appropriate screws. As far as possible, try to match the screwdriver tip to the screw slot to prevent damage to either of them.

Hand screwdrivers: these must have their tips filed true when there is any sign of rounding or damage. Small screwdrivers used on large screws are easily damaged. To reface a screwdriver, clamp it in a vice [vise], with scraps of wood to protect the wooden jaw linings if necessary. Use a flat metalwork or mill file and file the front end flat and square. Then trim each of the four sides in turn. If you must use a screwdriver as a chisel or a crowbar, to open paint cans and so on, keep an old one specially for the job, and you will have far less filing to do on your good ones.

Spiral ratchet screwdrivers: these need only the occasional drop or two of oil in the chuck sleeve. Pull the chuck sleeve as if inserting a bit and drop the oil in the small space at the front. The oil will work its way gradually back to the ratchet mechanism. Too much oil or grease on the grooved driving stem tends to carry grit back into the 'works' and wear them out. Better no oil at all than too much with these tools.

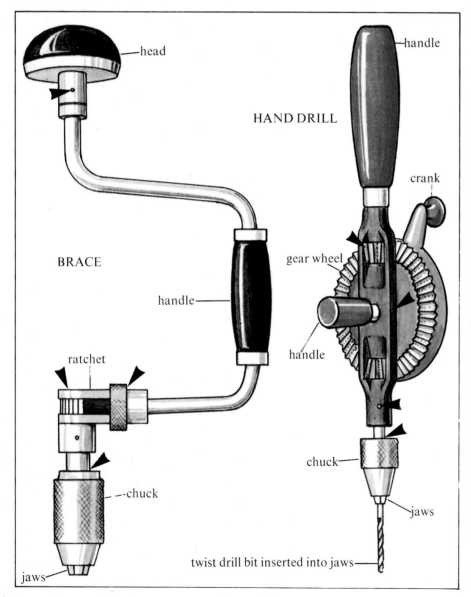

HAND DRILL

head

handle

crank

gear wheel

BRACE

handle

handle

ratchet

chuck

chuck

jaws

jaws

twist drill bit inserted into jaws

Left: *arrows indicate the parts to be lubricated. Use a household oil.*

Starting
with
Simple Repairs

Chair legs become wobbly or a back rest works loose. A table wobbles from side to side during lunch. Drawers stick or start to come unstuck. Hinges, castors, begin to work loose. These are some of the simple ailments from which old, or hard-used, furniture suffers and which are relatively easy to cure. Like a doctor with a patient, you first must establish what is causing the trouble; then common sense will tell you what to do.

However, a good doctor knows when the services of a specialist should be called on, just as the sensible home craftsman or woman can sense when it is wiser to have a piece of furniture repaired professionally, rather than attempt to put it right at home. This applies to any trouble you cannot clearly diagnose, and, of course, to any valuable antique. Where a repair is likely to mar a high finish or veneer which may be hard to match afterwards; where the repair means the reproduction of complex shapes or ornamentation; where you would need to buy specialist equipment out of all proportion to the potential saving, a professional job may make good sense. These, however, are special cases. A great number of the more common mending, tightening and easing jobs needed from time to time can be successfully carried out with basic tools and equipment. Start with a simple repair and build up your skills and confidence. The only way anyone ever gains experience is by actually tackling something.

Adhesives
Extra-strong, quick-setting modern adhesives have largely replaced the animal glues traditionally used by furniture makers. In some cases a modern glue works better than a nail in the right place. Cold pva woodworking adhesives [polyvinyl-acetate glues] set in 10-20 minutes, need clamping, and dry in 24 hours. Epoxy resin glues set so fast that you can sometimes hold a small repair together for a few minutes instead of clamping it. Resorcinol glue is the best adhesive for wood exposed to moisture. Consult the

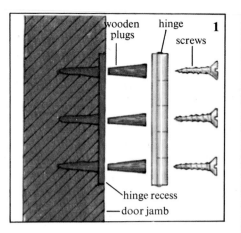

1. *Repairing a loose hinge with the use of dowel rods.*
Correcting uneven chair legs
2. *Check the amount to be cut off, using waste pieces of wood.*
3 & 4. *Saw off the excess lengths ensuring that if the legs are angled, they are cut horizontally.*

package instructions for application techniques. No adhesive will work in a dirty, damp, gappy joint.

Loose hinges and other hardware
It is a reasonably simple operation to replace or re-anchor hinges, locks and similar hardware. Wood shrinkage and leverage on screws exerted by, for example, opening and closing doors, combine to enlarge screw holes and make the hardware slide about or become detached. So long as the wood is not broken away at the edges, most loose screws can be firmly re-anchored. Start by taking the hinge or piece of hardware right off. Cut small pieces of dowel rod slightly longer than the screws and taper them by filing or sanding to make tiny plugs to fit into the screw holes. Tap them lightly into the holes and trim flush with the surface using a sharp knife or chisel. Place the hardware in position and make a mark for each hole. Use a hammer and nail punch or bradawl to make a small starting hole to guide the drill bit. Choose a drill bit the same size as the screw. Drill the holes deep enough to hold the screws. Replace the hardware. If the wood round the screw holes is badly chipped and broken, use a drill bit slightly larger than the holes and re-bore them. Use thicker dowel rods

to plug the holes and proceed as before.

Replacing castors
If the holes have become too large to hold the castor fitting, securely plug them with a piece of dowel cut to fit snugly and a little wood glue. Re-bore the holes and re-attach the castors. If the leg has split, carefully lever the castor out of its metal or plastic housing at the bottom of the leg with a screwdriver. Pry out the housing and remove it. Push the screwdriver into the hole in the leg and carefully lever the crack open. Squeeze glue into the crack. Clamp the crack tightly, protecting the wood with padding or softwood blocks if necessary, until the glue is hard. Clean the hole, hammer the housing back in place, re-fit the castor.

Uneven legs
Do not rely on a bit of folded paper to stop a chair or table wobbling because of an uneven leg. Check first whether it is the leg or the floor that is uneven. To do this, place the

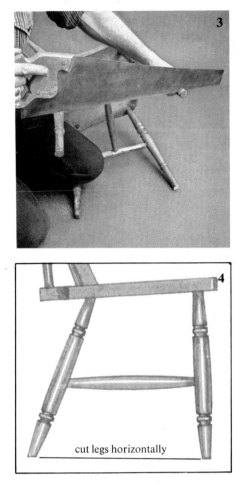

cut legs horizontally

without leaving too marked a line. Open the split carefully and squeeze or brush woodworking adhesive or glue into it as far as you can (pva [polyvinyl-acetate glue] adhesive can be bought in plastic bottles fitted with a handy nozzle). Smooth the adhesive into the split with a thin piece of waste wood or cardboard, working quickly as the adhesive dries fast. Wipe off any excess adhesive before clamping, as it is difficult to remove when dry. You may need some ingenuity to devise a clamp which will hold the mend together until the adhesive is set. You can use G [C]-clamps, protecting the wood with two scraps of wood. You can devise a kind of tourniquet with a clothes line and a piece of wood. You can use weights, a sash clamp, a portable vice [vise]. Apply firm pressure, but not too much or the mend will jackknife apart. Use wood filler to patch any gaps before re-polishing. Fresh breaks in legs of any shape can be glued together, but need strengthening with a connecting piece of dowel. First tap a panel pin [finishing nail] into one section of the break and file the head end sharp. Press this end into the other section of the break to get an exact mark where the dowel should go. Remove the pin [nail] and hand-drill a small hole in each part of the break, using a drill of the same diameter as the dowel for a snug fit. Round the ends of the dowel a little and make a narrow groove down its length to allow excess glue to escape. Dip one end in glue, tap into one hole, glue and tap the broken section in place, smearing a little glue on the broken surfaces.

Wood panels are not normally glued into their supporting grooves in the sides of cabinet furniture, to allow for expansion and contraction of the wood. It is often possible to re-glue joints between panels, using temporary screws or pins [nails] on the inside to wire or string the glued edges together until set. Panels can warp and split with age. If it is impossible to re-glue these, disguise narrow cracks with the right tone of wood filler (slightly darker than the raw wood).

piece of furniture on a surface you know to be level. A sheet of chipboard or masonite is likely to be level, since it is extremely stable and warp-proof. If the floor is uneven, simply move the chair. To correct uneven legs, all four legs must be cut to the same length, taking special note if the back legs are angled. Stand the chair on a flat surface. Pack small pieces of waste wood or cardboard under the short leg or legs until the chair stands evenly. Cut a bit of wood slightly thicker than the packing. With the wood held flat against the flat surface, mark its thickness on each of the four legs. Saw off the ends carefully, checking for squareness or angle. Clean up the cut ends with sandpaper.

Breaks, cracks, splits

Clean breaks in stretchers, rails, legs or splats of tables and chairs can often be repaired without taking the whole piece apart. Check first that the break is clean and that no pieces are missing, so that the edges will clamp together closely

Loose joints

Many loose joints are caused by the natural movement of the wood as it dries out over the years. As it dries, it shrinks: very little along the grain, but usually quite markedly across it. Mortises and dovetail slots widen out and the tenons and pins [nails] which fit them become narrower. Eventually, the ability of the animal glue (which has some elasticity) to accommodate the movement is worn out and the joint begins to loosen. If it goes unrepaired whilst strain is still put on it, some wood may well rub away so that the joint movement is increased still further. The main types of joints which you are more than likely to encounter are clearly detailed below.

Mortise and tenon joints

Dowel peg joints: these are where two pieces are held together by pieces of dowel. Usually the dowels are concealed, so that they are not visible on the surface of the piece. *Dovetail joints:* these are joints like the stub or blind tenon joint, which hides the tenon in the mortise; glued and wedged joints; mitred mortise and tenon joint. Most joints, if loose, can normally be knocked apart easily and re-glued or repaired. A few firm tugs on each part is sometimes sufficient, or the parts can be separated using a mallet and a scrap block of wood. Before attempting this, consider what other (undamaged) pieces will have to be removed to enable you to do this. If the damaged joint is, say, a horizontal bar in the middle of a chair back, any horizontal bar above the loose one will have to be removed. If, however, the broken piece is a cross bar between two chair legs, there may be enough 'give' between the legs to enable you to remove and re-fit the damaged one without taking the chair apart. Do not force the legs apart, however, as you may damage perfectly good joints in the rest of the chair. Damaged parts can be removed in the following way. Place a scrap block of wood on the piece to be removed, adjacent to and on the same side as the joint.

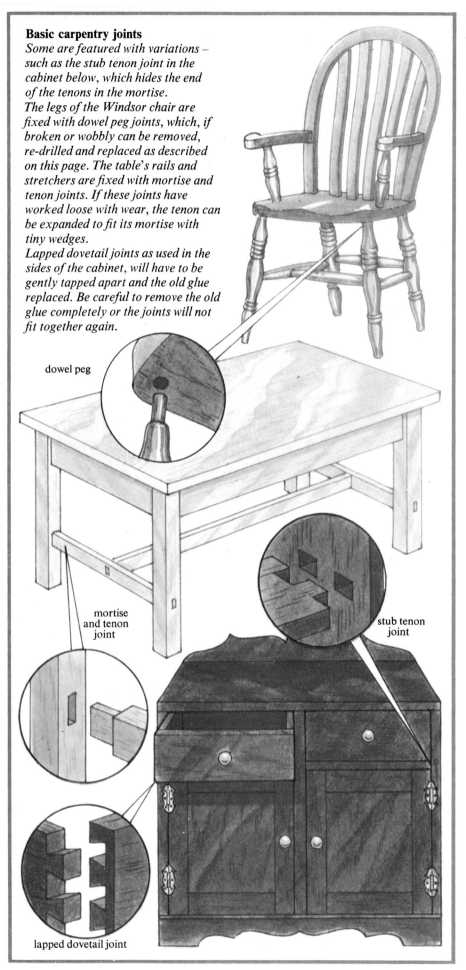

Basic carpentry joints

*Some are featured with variations –
such as the stub tenon joint in the
cabinet below, which hides the end
of the tenons in the mortise.*

*The legs of the Windsor chair are
fixed with dowel peg joints, which, if
broken or wobbly can be removed,
re-drilled and replaced as described
on this page. The table's rails and
stretchers are fixed with mortise and
tenon joints. If these joints have
worked loose with wear, the tenon can
be expanded to fit its mortise with
tiny wedges.*

*Lapped dovetail joints as used in the
sides of the cabinet, will have to be
gently tapped apart and the old glue
replaced. Be careful to remove the old
glue completely or the joints will not
fit together again.*

dowel peg

mortise
and tenon
joint

stub tenon
joint

lapped dovetail joint

Take a firm hold of the part to be
removed and hammer the block
against the adjoining piece of wood
with a mallet until the joint comes
apart. You many need someone to
help you with this.

If the piece has broken in the
joint, it will have to be cut from the
rest of the piece. The joint may be
held with dowels. In this case, slide
a chisel into the joint and, when the
point of the chisel reaches the
dowel, tap the top of the handle
firmly with a mallet to break the
dowels. Sand down the ends of the
dowels until they are flush with the
surfaces, and drill the broken
dowels from both holes. Measure
the depth of the dowel holes, using
a pencil as a gauge. Cut new pieces
of dowel, the same diameter as the
holes, fractionally shorter than the
depth. Glue and tap the dowels into
one set of holes. Glue protruding
dowels and the other holes. Fix
together and clamp the joint
together until the glue is set.

Tenons going right through a
frame component, for example,
will show as an oblong of con-
trasting grain on the other side of
the component. In many cases these
can be expanded to fit their mortise
by judicious wedging. Wedges
should be cut from hardwood
without any pronounced grain.
Beech and mahogany are very
suitable.

Enlarging a tenon: make two or
three narrow wedges cut to a gentle
taper, the width of the end section
of the tenon. Cut slots across the
tenon's width with a sharp chisel
slightly narrower than the tenon.
Cover the wedges with glue and tap
them into the slots with a light hammer and a piece of scrap wood.
(Two or three little wedges are
better than a single wide one.)
Leave the wedges until the glue has
set, then chisel them flush with the
original surface. Make sure that the
tenon is pushed right the way home
while the wedges are tapped in.

Dovetail and stub or blind tenon
joints cannot be treated in this way.
However, both kinds of joint can
be knocked gently apart and re-
glued.

Fox-wedging: once taken apart, the

stub or blind tenon can have small saw slits made in it to accommodate tiny wedges, which are glued, partially inserted into the slits and finally forced home to spread the tenon back to size as the joint is clamped together again. It is highly effective, although it holds some risk for the haphazard worker, since there is little chance of a second try if the first should fail. Fortunately, failures are easy to avoid.

Oversize wedges are usually the root of any trouble, so take care in estimating the total extent of increase in size required to make a tenon fit its mortise. Do this by cutting saw slits a little longer than would seem strictly necessary; shaping the wedges to a gradual taper and precise length (a bit shorter than the saw slits, which should not extend more than half-way down the tenon). Measure the wedges at the thick ends to make sure that their total thickness is not much greater than the spread you want in the tenon. Remember that it must be *fractionally* greater for the repair to work, and that you cannot cut down the wedges after the repaired joint has been clamped together. The harder the furniture wood, the smaller the spread in the joint needs to be.

Since you have to take a complete joint apart, you will have to put adhesive over all the mating parts—that is, the parts which go inside each other, not just on the wedges. It is as well to use glue of the same general type as that already used, because the wood will have become impregnated with it. Traces of brownish 'toffee' indicate a gelatine or animal glue, whitish deposits a modern resin adhesive.

Remove old glue from angles and corners before you re-assemble a joint. Glue will be squeezed out as you re-clamp. You can leave an animal glue until it has hardened before chipping off the surplus, but most modern kinds set very hard indeed, so wipe the surfaces clean with a damp rag as soon as clamping is complete. Clamping time is measured from the first application of the glue and the setting speed may be shorter than the instructions say when you are working in a warm room. Do a glueless practice assembly whenever you can. Panel pins [finishing nails] can sometimes be used to hold the joint together while glue sets, but you have to be able to hold the joints tightly until the pins [nails] are in place.

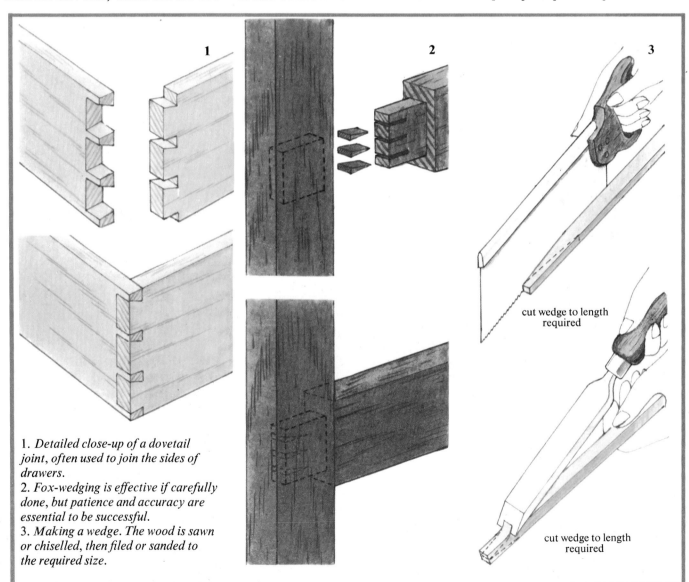

1. *Detailed close-up of a dovetail joint, often used to join the sides of drawers.*
2. *Fox-wedging is effective if carefully done, but patience and accuracy are essential to be successful.*
3. *Making a wedge. The wood is sawn or chiselled, then filed or sanded to the required size.*

cut wedge to length required

cut wedge to length required

Treating
Wood Well

A great deal of old furniture has been badly treated over the years although structurally it may still be in good condition. Do not reject a junk shop bargain, or a hand-me-down from a relative just because its surface is battered. There are few surface finishes on solid old furniture which cannot be restored with a bit of practice and persistence. People tend to pass over old—but not antique or particularly valuable—pieces of furniture. Congealed or dirty paint, damaged var-

nish, scratches, cigarette burns, watermarks, delicate details or a fine basic wood obscured by layers of one finish or another—all can be cleaned, stripped if necessary, and vastly improved. And it is marvellous how well solid wood will come up and take on a new life with some hard work and at a minimum cost. Try your hand at a small unimportant piece first—perhaps an old coffee table—then see if you can apply your restoring touch to a neglected treasure which you will be

Above: *amidst a junk shop's jumble, grubby and neglected, it is easy to overlook these attractive pieces.*

proud to take into your home.

If you think the piece you are concerned with may be antique and of some value, then be sure to have an expert look at it before you do anything at all to it. It is quite possible that it may be worth more in its original state, even if damaged, than it would be after anyone but an expert had tried to restore it.

The patina, that deep surface built up over years of loving care and painstaking polishing, cannot be replaced by short-cut modern methods: so hesitate before you destroy it. If you think that a painted piece may have a distinguished pedigree, get an expert to check.

The first essential in renovating old furniture is to clean it gently and thoroughly. Once you have done this, you will have a better idea of the quality of the wood it is made of, and you can then decide what restoration method is best suited to your find, or make up your mind to leave well alone. Indeed, once the dirt is removed, a good polish may be all the piece requires.

Cleaning furniture

Never pour vast amounts of soapy water recklessly over anything made of wood. It may well become so waterlogged that it warps or rots. Fine surfaces, particularly veneered ones, can be damaged beyond repair. First, if your piece is only lightly soiled, a well squeezed-out chamois leather and mild detergent may be enough to clean it. Wipe dry immediately afterwards. Heavy, dirty wax polish build-up can be cleaned with a rag damped in turpentine or white spirit [mineral spirits]. Be careful with veneered areas, particularly ones which have intricate patterns of decorative wood pieces. These are very thin and probably fixed in place with an animal glue. If you let water or a solvent seep beneath the veneer, the adhesive can dissolve, the veneer curl up, and you will have a tricky restoration job on your hands. If you are not sure if the piece is actually covered in thin sheets of veneer, take a close look at the edge of a flat surface: you can normally see where the veneer is joined. This 'go carefully' warning also applies to decorative bandings, inlays of ivory, ebony and other materials.

You can treat a plain solid wood piece of furniture a little more roughly; the finest steel wool dipped in turpentine will remove polish build-up. A mildly abrasive powder sprinkled on a slightly damp cloth, helps clean up non-precious pieces. Once the piece is cleaned, you may find that all you need to do is to polish it again or revive the surface with one of the methods in the following pages. On the other hand, you may get a good look at scratches, dents and other disfigurements that you want to deal with first.

Old finishes

Much old furniture was finished with materials that are no longer normally used. It may, therefore, be tricky to patch up an old finish with modern materials. There are no absolute directions for this. In general, attempting to touch up small patches is not as easy for a beginner as stripping a piece down to the wood and applying a new modern finish. Certain techniques, such as French polishing, need practice.

There are two main categories of surface finishes. First, those where colour and patina have been achieved by years of oiling, waxing and elbow grease, either on stained or natural wood; and second, applied finishes such as varnish, French polish or paint.

Oiled finishes or stains

These darken wood but do not cover the grain or texture. When built up over the years, the finish is quite tough, non-glossy and water resistant. Oak, deal and various pine and beech furniture was traditionally finished with oil and wax, or with oil and a turpentine-gum based varnish. The latter finish is not used today. Softwoods in general were not suitable for oiling. You can tell if a piece has no applied finish except wax and oil by rubbing a small area with turpentine and a soft cloth. A few rubs will take the spot down to the bare wood.

Wax finishes

These have always been traditionally made from a mixture of beeswax and turpentine, sometimes with added carnauba or candle wax. Modern wax finishes are made with silicone ingredients and are more resistant to surface and water marking. A wax finish is not a particularly durable finish on raw wood, and if used, the surface should first be sealed with a modern varnish. Wax polish is, however, excellent as a finish for other finishes, and for enhancing French polish. If, after your turpentine test, a polished surface is still visible, rub on a little methylated spirits [denatured alcohol]. If the surface softens and goes sticky it has been French polished.

French polish

This is a very traditional finish often found on antique and more recent furniture. It is made of shellac which is dissolved in methylated spirits [denatured alcohol], but its characteristic mirror-like surface is achieved by the actual application technique. It is a fine, grain-enhancing finish, but can be easily marked by liquids or heat.

Varnishes

These are characterized by a hard glossy, usually transparent finish on the wood. There are numerous different types of varnishes—some based on natural wood resins, others on shellac and a volatile spirit mixture, others on cellulose and other synthetics. Most mass-produced furniture made within the last 50 years (except good quality reproduction furniture and that with a polyurethane resin or melamine resin finish) was covered with a cellulose-based varnish. This can be identified by the thick, brownish, rather layered appearance of the surface coating.

Modern synthetic surface finishes

Often polyurethane resins, give the same effect as the older varnishes. They are more resistant to heat, water, scratching and staining than either cellulose varnishes or French polish. They are also harder to remove.

A further test for ascertaining the type of finish, is to scrape a small, unnoticeable patch with a razor blade. French polish should pro-

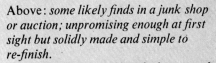

Above: *some likely finds in a junk shop or auction; unpromising enough at first sight but solidly made and simple to re-finish.*
Painstakingly stripped to the bare wood, each was given a special treatment to highlight the natural look. The chair was clear-finished (some varnish still remains in the grain); the cupboard was limed and clear-finished; the settle was treated with diluted stain for a new colour tone.

duce very thin shavings or curls; oil varnishes produce thicker shavings; and cellulose varnishes will only scrape to powder.

Reviving the surface

After cleaning you may find that a French polished surface is intact but that you want to give it a new lease of life. Restore its gloss with a mixture of five parts methylated spirits [denatured alcohol], two parts boiled linseed oil, one part real turpentine. Apply this sparingly to the surface on a soft cloth pad, working with a steady, continuous circular or 'figure of eight' motion, never allowing the cloth to stay still on the surface. Make sure you treat the corners and edges as well as the centre of the piece as these areas show wear and dirt most. Buff up the surface with a clean dry cloth to bring up the shine.

If the French polished surface has split into hair-line cracks or has light scratches on it, you can try 're-amalgamating' or spot finishing it. Rub first with the mixture as above, then paint it over lightly and swiftly with methylated spirits [denatured alcohol]. This will dissolve the shellac in the finish slightly and, with luck, will make it run together to give a smooth surface. Leave the surface to re-set completely before you check your success, then rub with a soft cloth. If your touch has not been delicate enough to smooth out the blemishes without disturbing the surface, you will have to remove the existing French polish completely and re-surface the piece with French polish or a more modern finish.

Very badly blemished French polished surfaces can sometimes be renovated by using 'padding lacquer' or French polish finish restorer which gives a new surface at the same time as it fills cracks. Pour the liquid into a saucer. Make up a pad of soft, lint-free material to fit your hand comfortably and dip it into the lacquer. Apply to the surface in continuous, circular movements, without pausing or lifting the pad (except at the edges of the piece), as this will leave a mark. Gradually increase the pressure.

The friction caused by the rubbing sets the polish, but if you rub too hard at first, the pad will stick. Repeat the application until the surface is uniformly smooth. The process takes practice. If the finish is too glossy for your taste, you can rub it down to a matt or satin finish with the finest steel wool and a dab of furniture polish. As the process and skills needed closely resemble French polishing, you might prefer to remove the blemished surface completely and learn to apply a French polish finish in the traditional way, rather than trying to renovate the surface in a 'second-best' way.

Blemished surfaces
Scratches
Fine scratches can be masked with store-bought scratch-covering polishes, or sometimes rubbed out with a fine abrasive powder damped with linseed oil. Do this very gently so as not to cut the finish and re-polish afterwards.

Cracks
Melt a few scrapings of beeswax in a spoon, hold over a candle and tint it to match the wood tone with a little artists' oil colour. Burnt sienna has the reddish tinge of mahogany, raw umber the yellowish tint of pine, burnt umber a blackish-brown tone which goes well with an age-darkened wood. Pour or rub the mixture into the crack and when hard, smooth the surface with a razor blade. A dab of shellac will protect the surface. This

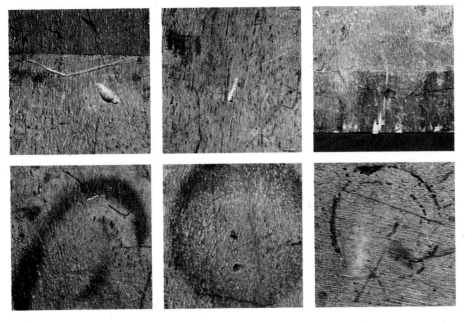

Right: *typical surface damage and wear and tear on old furniture. Dents, scratches, burns, black marks can all be remedied with a little care.*
Below: *common softwoods showing the colour change before and after finishing.*
Left to right: *Parana pine, Siberian pine, British Columbian pine, Swedish pine and Western red cedar.*

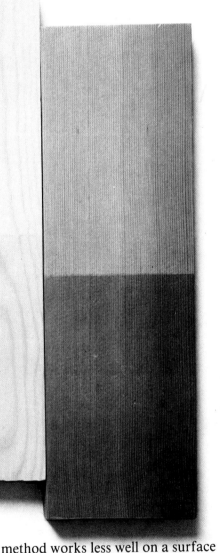

method works less well on a surface which will get daily wear. You can buy wood filler pastes, tinted to most wood tones, which can be pressed into the crack, allowed to harden, and then rubbed smooth with fine sandpaper to give a harder surface. You can disguise the repair with a fingerprint of toning oil paint, and when dry, a touch of shellac for protection.

Heat marks
Heat makes white patches on cellulose and French polished finishes. Rub with a mixture of one

part real turpentine and one part linseed oil. Clean off with vinegar and repeat the process if necessary. You can also try moistened cigar ash, a paste of linseed oil and rottenstone (available at paint stores) or an abrasive store-bought ring remover.

Black marks
These are usually caused by water which has seeped under the surface finish, possibly from flower vases or wet glasses. You will need to remove the finish over them. As the older finishes are usually vulnerable to water, you will find that turpentine will remove wax or oil finishes, methylated spirits [denatured alcohol] will remove French polish, varnish remover or strong ammonia will take off a cellulose finish. You can then try to abrade the black mark with finest sandpaper.

Dents
These can sometimes be raised with a damp rag and a warm iron. Lay the rag over the dent and place the iron on top. The moisture helps the surface to swell and level out. Be very careful not to scorch the surface with an iron that has got too hot or stands in place too long. Be careful to protect the surrounding surface, particularly if it is veneered.

Burns
Shallow cigarette burns can be

rubbed away with sandpaper or moistened cigar ash. Use a fine paper and a gentle touch. Re-touch the colour with a fingerprint of artists' oil colour, the right coloured shoe polish or a store-bought tinted scratch covering polish or lacquer stick. Re-polish carefully, when the piece is dry.

Alcohol
This is a solvent which will damage most old finishes, so wipe up spills immediately and leave the surface to set. If a French polished surface has been marked, try the techniques mentioned before. The mildest abrasive (cigar ash is traditional) may help, followed by an all-over gentle polishing with furniture wax. Bad marks mean that the whole surface must be removed and a new French or other polish applied.

Stripping the finish
This can be done in one of three ways: mechanical, heat or chemical. Remember that stripping the finish from a damaged area, removing the blemishes and renewing the finish, does not necessarily mean stripping the entire piece. Probably only the surface which needs attention will have to be stripped. Tops of furniture pieces generally have the most wear and damage and it is often a practical idea to strip and re-finish them with a more modern, less vulnerable coating.

Mechanical stripping

You will need:

- Double-bladed scraper, cabinet scraper or improvised scraping edge, such as a suitably sized piece of broken glass (break up a smallish bottle inside a plastic bag and choose a suitable piece, binding the edges you will hold with adhesive tape).

For small damaged areas use a double-bladed scraper. Use the serrated edge to score the paint film and shave off the paint surface with the other blade, using the scraper like a plane.

Flat surfaces can be scraped with a cabinet scraper, which is a simple, inexpensive tool consisting of a piece of sheet steel about 10×5 cm (4×2 in). One side of this is absolutely straight, and each of the square edges of this straight side is sharpened with a flat file at an angle of about 20°, or turned over with a screwdriver to give it a burr so that it cuts cleanly through the varnish. To use the scraper, hold it with both hands, one at each side, with the sharpened side underneath. Press your thumbs against the middle bending the metal into a slight curve, then scrape the surface by pushing the tool away from you, working always along the grain of the wood, not across it. For scraping curves and mouldings, a piece of broken glass of a suitable shape can be useful. For any area which a scraper will not reach, use coarse or medium, and then fine steel wool. For holes and corners, try an old but sharp wood rasp or chisel.

Heat stripping

Warning: the following process should only be undertaken with extreme caution and used only on surfaces that are going to be repainted.

You will need:

- 'Handyman' blowtorch (the experienced can use a commercial bottle gas or butane blowtorch)
- Broad stripping knife, 75 mm (3 in)
- Dust sheet (drop cloth) to protect

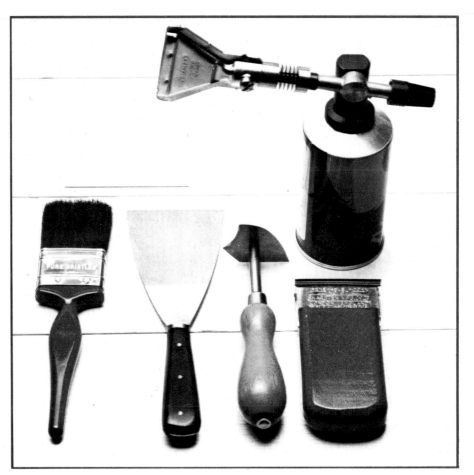

Stripping tools.
Top left: *cabinet scraper*. Top right: *blowtorch*. Bottom row, left to right: *paintbrush, stripping knife, multi-purpose shavehook [paint scraper], double-bladed scraper.*

working area
- Container (not plastic) for the paint scraps
- You will also find white spirit [mineral spirits] useful for cleaning surfaces and medium glasspaper [emery cloth] useful for keying clean surfaces

This is the quickest way of stripping paint but, unless you are very skilled, it is suitable only for areas you intend to paint, as it is almost impossible to take the paint off the surface without charring it a little here and there. The paint is softened by heat from the blowtorch. Different fittings are available, ranging from pin-point flame to a fan spread for large areas. Choose the most appropriate fitting for your surface.

Always treat your blowtorch and the flame it produces with great respect and use a sheet of newspaper or a dust-sheet [drop cloth], to protect the floor or work surface from hot paint strippings. If you are trying the blowtorch for the first time, practise on a flat surface first. Difficult areas such as

mouldings or areas round mirrors are best stripped by another method, as wood can be damaged and glass cracked by the heat of the flame, particularly if it is too large or kept stationary.

Play the flame carefully back and forth across the surface and as the paint shrivels, scrape it with the scraper held at an angle (this prevents the softened paint from falling on your hands). Put the paint scraps into the waste container.

Get into the habit of turning the flame away from the surface while you are scraping: this helps to prevent accidental surface burns and avoids setting the paint scraps alight.

Chemical stripping
You will need:

- Paint stripper—use a store-bought paint stripper, available as a liquid or jelly, or the appropriate solvent for your surface as detailed. Consult your retailer as to the most appropriate one.

- An old 50 mm (2 in) brush for applying stripper. A toothbrush is useful for working stripper into crevices
- Scraper for flat areas; multi-purpose shavehook [paint scraper] for tricky areas
- Neutralizer and rag, if necessary (see instructions on paint stripper label)
- Protection for hands and eyes
- A thick layer of newspaper to protect working area
- Container (not plastic) for the paint scraps

Methylated spirits [denatured alcohol] will soften French polish. Rubbing with turpentine and a rag will remove waxed and oiled finishes. You will need a modern commercial stripper for layers of paint, varnish and most modern finishes. For fine surfaces, veneers and marquetry areas, use a stripper containing turpentine as a finishing clean-up rather than water to avoid damage.

Using an old brush, carefully apply the stripper in smallish sections to the surface, working it well into crevices and cracks. Leave the chemical to soften and 'lift' the paint—do not be in a hurry. When the treated area bubbles and curls, scrape the surface gently with a shavehook or scraper. Push the scraper away from you and collect the highly caustic paint scraps in a container as you go. Strippers rarely take off a layered surface down to the wood in the first application but tend to shrivel it layer by layer. Several applications may be needed. Remember to let the stripper do its work; do not be too eager to attack it with the scraper.

Wrap and put the scrapings in the dustbin [garbage can] as soon as possible, out of reach of children and animals. Wear old clothes, gloves, protect eyes if necessary and work outside or leave windows open. Avoid breathing the chemical fumes. Wash off any spilt stripper immediately with plenty of water.

When the surface is stripped down to the wood, clean it in the way described in the manufacturer's instructions. Finally, when the surface is dry, go over it with fine steel wool or sandpaper. This removes all traces of the stripper and prevents any residue from reacting with the new applied surface.

Antique dealers strip solid hardwood and pine furniture by immersing pieces in tanks of trisodium phosphate (a chemical paint solvent) solution heated to 66°C (150°F). If you have a suitable tank, mix about two and one half cupfuls of the chemical per gallon of hot water to make a saturated solution (one in which no more of the chemical will dissolve). Immerse the object, gently heat the solution and the surfacing will come off. Rinse well with clean water and allow to dry slowly and thoroughly before re-finishing. The chemical is cheap and relatively non-caustic, but always protect skin and clothing. Be sure, too, that your piece of furniture will stand the process, which is bound to swell the wood, loosen old glues and which can cause the whole piece to fall apart.

Left: *when stripping paint, protect your hands and the work surface and give the stripper time to work.* Below: *the results are well worth the effort.*

Various ways of stripping wood are illustrated here; choose the gentlest for your most precious pieces and for pieces you plan to re-finish with a clear varnish.

1. You can carefully lift old varnish and lacquer with a cabinet scraper. This is the gentlest, most painstaking way of removing a surface.

2. A double-bladed scraper is convenient for small areas and furniture that is less than precious.

3. Chemical stripper will soften and loosen paint and varnish so that you can gently scrape it off. Use the shavehook [paint scraper] for tricky areas, including mouldings and corners.

4. Use a blowtorch for thickly encrusted paint on a piece you plan to re-paint. Remember that the flame size must be carefully adjusted for melting the paint without charring the wood.

5. Quickly lift off the paint as it shrivels with a broad stripping knife.

A quick, drastic, messy but inexpensive method of stripping off an old finish is to take the relevant article outside on a warm day—over 21°C (70°F)—place it on a concreted area away from grass or flowers and swab it down with caustic soda solution. Use one can of crystals to one quart of water, or follow instructions on can, adding crystals to water, *not* vice versa or the mixture will spit. Wear overalls, rubber gloves and glasses and apply the solution with a mop of some kind. Leave the surface to soften and then hose it down. A little vinegar neutralizes the caustic soda. This treatment will darken the wood and is only suitable for very solid pieces such as doors. Be *sure* to hose the working area thoroughly after completing the job as soda crystals can damage children's bare feet and animals' paws.

Bleaching

When you get down to the wood you may find that the stripping process has darkened it, or you may simply like the look of a lighter wood tone. It is possible to lighten the colour somewhat. A strong domestic bleach can work on a sturdy, non-precious piece of furniture. For a better piece, use a store-bought wood bleach and follow the manfacturer's instructions exactly, especially concerning how long you should leave the bleach on the wood. Stripping and bleaching processes will raise the grain of the wood, especially if it is a softwood, so when the job is complete and the piece thoroughly dry, you should rub carefully along the grain with medium sandpaper before attempting to put a new finish. Remember never to over-wet valuable, veneered or decorated pieces of furniture.

Alternative wood finishes

There are various different treatments for bare wood which can enhance the colour, or the wood grain, or form a protective layer over the wood. When you have stripped and renovated your piece you might consider giving the wood a new look. These methods also work well on new, untreated wood surfaces.

Liming

This process is carried out on oak. The purpose of the process is to emphasize the full beauty of the wood grain. It involves filling all the surface pores and grain lines with finely ground lime so that they show up in paler contrast to the wood.

There are two additional benefits to be gained from liming: the filling of the oak surface makes it a good deal smoother than if it had been left untreated. In addition, the lime and water paste used for the process partially bleaches the natural yellowness out of the wood, leaving it a more attractive grey–brown.

Lime does not react well to finishing or sealing processes, so if you want to add a final protective finish to the furniture it is advisable to forget the authentic process and use a white wood filler or an alternative filler.

Plaster-based fillers, used for stopping holes in walls and ceilings, can give a similar finish. You can also get the look by mixing titanium white powder with a store-bought modern transparent grain filler. Remember that these fillers do not have the bleaching effect of lime.

Liming is most effective on woods which have an open-grained surface, such as oak, elm and many mahoganies. Beech and close-grained fruitwoods do not take the finish so well. To open up the grain and make it more pronounced, use a fine wire brush in the direction of the grain. Work gently and carefully so as not to damage the wood fibres.

You will need:

- Lime (garden lime available from garden centres and garden equipment suppliers)
- Water. Note: lime is caustic so wear rubber gloves, eye protection and protect your working area. Or use a suggested alternative filler
- Coarse cloth rags, fine steel wool, fine grade sandpaper

- Fine wire brush—optional
- Rubber gloves and other protective clothing
- White French polish
- White wax polish: add zinc white powder to wax polish to enhance the contrast of the white deposit in the wood grain

Prepare the wood surface, making sure that it is clean and free from dust. Accentuate the grain by using the wire brush, if necessary.

Put 1 kg (2 lb 3 oz) of hydrated lime in 3.5 litres (6 pints or 1 U.S. gallon) of water. Mix to a stiffish paste. This quantity should be enough to treat a fairly large table. Using a coarse cloth or steel wool, rub the paste into the wood. Use a circular motion to ensure that all the surface pores and grain indentations are filled. When the lime is semi-dry, wipe off any surplus with a cloth, working across the grain. When the lime is thoroughly dry, smooth the surface with fine grade sandpaper. Wipe with a clean cloth. Apply a coat of white French polish with a rag or brush. Rub up with polish when completely dry.

If you are using an alternative filler, mix to a paste with water and apply as the lime. Sand and wipe down as before, then add a modern sealing finish. A water-clear finish will look best. Bear in mind that most polyurethane finishes, although labelled 'clear', are slightly brownish in colour when applied.

Fuming

Note: *This project should not be undertaken by a complete beginner as the method is very exacting.* The established method of changing the tone of natural wood by fuming, involves exposing the bare wood to fumes given off by certain chemicals—usually ammonia. Used mostly for oak, it turns the wood a deep brown. It is difficult to control the colour, which can vary from light to an almost black tone. Fumes given off by many chemicals will darken wood but it is hard to predict or control the effect. Another problem involves the finishes that can be applied after the toning process has been carried

Pickling a pine cabinet by painting on nitric acid.   *The acid is neutralized with a soda water solution.*

The cabinet with a pickled finish.

out. It is difficult to remove chemical residues which the process leaves in the wood. So the final effect is seldom predictable.

The gas from ammonia is most commonly used for this process. It does not remain in the wood once its work is done so has less effect on the finish you want to apply. It does not raise and roughen the grain fibres too markedly, nor does it need any neutralizing process before the wood is finished.

Method: prepare an airtight fuming box or chamber, large enough to stand the piece of furniture in. Obviously, large pieces of furniture cannot be fumed at home. Remember that the wood must not touch the ammonia, so the piece must stand on a grid or similar support, or be suspended in some way. The ammonia is placed in a shallow receptacle and the fumes which rise from it do the work. The effect depends on how efficiently the fumes are trapped so that they do their utmost to the wood before escaping. It is most useful when you wish to repair a piece of fumed furniture—the new wood can be fumed to tone in with the older piece before you begin the renovation. Good ventilation is essential. Work in an outbuilding, or preferably out of doors.

You will need:
- A concentrated solution of ammonia
- Receptacles for the ammonia —two or three saucers for example
- Something to make a grid to hold the furniture, or the means to suspend it in the container
- A large airtight container

Pour ammonia into the receptacle. Be careful not to inhale the fumes or spill it on your skin. Place the piece of furniture or wood over the container of ammonia. Make the container as airtight as you can. Keep checking the wood until it is toned to the shade you desire, then remove from the fumes. You can get a deep-toned look by 'sponging' the ammonia on to the wood with a cloth. It will give a deeper shade

than if the wood is fumed. Be sure to wear rubber gloves and work in a well-ventilated place.

Pickled finish

This term can be applied to more than one finishing technique. At one time pine furniture was treated with plaster of Paris to make it smooth enough for painting. This remained in the grain after the painted finish was stripped off. The 'pickle' used to remove deteriorating paint did not affect the 'spackle', as the plaster of Paris was called. Consequently, the spackle remained in the broad, spring growth rings of the wood, accentuating the natural grain pattern. Any white powdery residues in the grain were difficult to remove completely and helped to accentuate it.

Today, a pickled finish is produced on pine by dilute nitric acid painted on to the wood. This deepens the natural colour, improving the contrast between the different grain textures, and can be used on other softwoods.

You will need:
- A dilute solution of nitric acid—two parts acid to eight parts water. Note: although the strength of acid solution is only 20 per cent nitric acid, it is still a

dangerous chemical to handle or to have about the house. Ideally, you should buy it diluted to the required strength but if you have to make up the solution yourself, always add the acid to the water a little at a time, so that the heat generated is dispersed more safely. Never add water to the acid; the heat generated on mixing is enough to make the water 'boil' and splutter and splash. Wash off any splashes immediately with lots of water.
- Glass or porcelain container for the acid
- An old paintbrush
- Washing soda
- Finest grade sandpaper

The wood should be clean and dry. Working along the grain, apply the acid solution as evenly as possible with a brush. Once you have the shade you want, neutralize the acid with a strong solution of washing soda and water—two parts soda to one part water. Rinse with clean water. The moisture in the process tends to raise the wood grain, so the surface must be lightly smoothed with sandpaper when thoroughly dry.

Below left: get an unusual wood finish by carefully scorching with a blowtorch. Right: charred rings are brushed out.

Above: *two cans of coloured stain intermixed, give an unusual look to a whitewood chest.*

are transparent, so the grain of the wood shows through after the tone is absorbed. Depth of colour is built up with several even applications.

Water-based stains: these come in powder form to be mixed with water. They are easy to apply with rag or brush, penetrate quite deeply and do not fade easily. Water raises the wood grain so the piece must be allowed to dry and be rubbed down smoothly with sandpaper between each application. Any modern or traditional finish may be applied over a water-based stain.

Oil-based stains: these contain turpentine, white spirit [mineral spirits], naptha, benzene or similar products. These stains do not raise the grain of the wood. The colour can be modified after application by rubbing down the surface with the basic solvent in the stain. These oil-based stains may 'bleed' through a subsequent finishing coat and need first to be sealed with a coat of thinned shellac varnish.

Spirit-based stains: these are based on methylated spirits [denatured alcohol]. They are penetrating, dry extremely fast, but may fade on prolonged exposure to daylight. Like oil-based stains, they do not raise the grain of the wood. You will need to apply an oil-based finishing coat over a spirit-based stain. These stains can also be added to French polish to tint it to the exact shade you want. The only problem you will find in staining wood is getting the tone even. Do not hurry the work and test the colour effect on an unnoticeable part first, before proceeeding.

Scorching

The colour and grain in pine and similar softwoods can be accentuated by lightly scorching the wood surface with a blowtorch. You will get an even effect by attaching a fishtail nozzle. The softer parts of the grain char more readily than the harder. Brush with a wire brush along the grain. This removes the charred areas and accentuates the grain contrast even more

strongly. The surface can then be sealed with a modern finish. Variations can be achieved by painting on a thin coat of oil-based paint and wiping the excess off with a rag before it is thoroughly dry. A deeper tone remains in the wire-brushed areas. Grey paint will give a driftwood effect, yellow or tan paint a blond shade.

Staining—store-bought stains

Wood stains: these are available in a variety of solvents in a wide range of colours to give a natural or colourful decorative look. The stains

Staining—home-made stains

Mahogany: bichromate of potash crystals dissolved in water will darken mahogany. Make a concentrated solution —$10\frac{1}{2}$ oz crystals to 9 L (2 gal or $2\frac{1}{2}$ U.S. gal.) and dilute it as required, always testing on a hidden spot and waiting until it is thoroughly dry before applying it to the surface. The stain darkens as it dries.

Oak: Vandyke brown or walnut crystals make an ideal oak stain, when completely dissolved in water with a little strong ammonia.

Bismark brown makes a reddish stain which is useful for giving other stains a warmer look.

Ebony: black aniline dye is best for retouching ebony.

Selecting the stain
If you want to use a natural-looking finish to light woods, see light finishes below. If you wish to stain a fairly evenly-coloured piece with all traces of old finish or varnish removed, consider water-based or penetrating oil stains. Oil stains are particularly good when re-finishing furniture, as they can be applied over existing stains, whereas water-based stains cannot. If, when re-finishing, you find that your piece is made up of different types of wood and you want an all-over effect, the masking properties of pigmented oil stains are ideal. For small patches and re-touching over varnished surfaces, try a spirit stain. For a brightly coloured look, varnish stains will give quick results.

Choosing the colour: when a stain is labelled 'light oak', 'mahogany' and so on, this is only an indication of the colour tone and it may well not be the exact colour you want. You can mix colours of the same brand and type, and you can dilute them with the appropriate solvent to get the effect you want.

There are other factors which will influence the final result. First, with the exception of pigmented oil stains, stains are transparent, so the colour of the wood underneath (as well as its texture) will affect the outcome. Also, the finish you use over the stain to seal the surface will affect the colour, be it wax, oil, varnish or shellac. Usually the colour will be deepened and enriched. You cannot lighten wood with stain, so if, after cleaning off all the dirt, the wood is still too dark, you will need to bleach it, then colour the bleached wood.

Testing: always test the colour somewhere hidden from view on the piece and also add the finish to see how it alters the colour.

Sanding: if sanding before staining, use the same grade sandpaper all over, as the surface of the wood

affects the amount of colour absorbed.

Avoiding streaks: some woods, especially soft woods like pine, have soft, porous areas which absorb more colour than the rest. When these are stained without the necessary precautions, the result is an unattractive, wildly-streaked grain. To prevent this, apply a wash coat to seal off the porous parts before using any stain.

Shellac wash coat: coat the wood with a very dilute solution of shellac—about one part shellac to six of methylated spirits [denatured alcohol]. Use white shellac on light woods, orange shellac on dark. You can use French polish or button polish but add less methylated spirits [denatured alcohol]. Allow to dry before using stain.

Oil wash: brush on a coat of one part boiled linseed oil mixed with three parts turpentine. Dry for at least a day before staining.

End grain: the grain at the end of a piece of wood tends to absorb more colour so treat with one of the above washes first.

Above: *a standard chair need not have a standard look. Bleaching can lighten the colour attractively, and staining can add a new deeper tone.*

Light finishes: chemical treatments, such as 'pickling', painting with household ammonia or stripping with caustic soda will give the look of natural ageing rather than stain. There is also a simple finish which will leave your pine furniture with the fashionable 'un-finished' look, which is so costly to buy and so easy to do. It is also a good way to finish stripped doors and woodwork.

All you need is a penetrating wood sealer; floor sealer will do. You can use the sealer as it is or tint it slightly with a very little raw or burnt umber artists' oil colour. Simply apply the sealer copiously all over the wood so that there is enough to soak in and still plenty left on the surface. Leave for ten minutes and then rub off with a cloth. When thoroughly dry—after about five hours—go over the surface with fine steel wool and then wax.

45

Restoring the Glow to Furniture

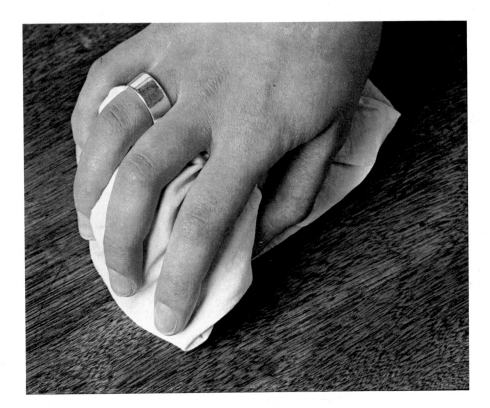

Your buy is home, clean and dry. Now all it needs is a little polish. Great-grandma made her own, that is why those heirlooms look so well cared for. Traditional beeswax polishes can be simply made in an ordinary kitchen without special equipment.

Bees were probably the first creatures kept by man, and over the centuries provided many of the necessities of man's existence: honey for food and medicine; mead for wine; wax to dip candles, fill cracks in the roof and polish tables and chairs. Today, honey is still widely available but beeswax, like many other natural products, has become expensive and is considered a luxury item. This is largely due to the development of synthetic furniture-care products, which, although less expensive, do not necessarily improve on the natural products. Luckily the old, time-honoured beeswax recipes are still with us, and although the materials are no longer inexpensive, the resulting polish is a superior product and the cost is less than that of a similar type of polish bought in a shop.

What is beeswax?
Bees make honey and wax. Under their tiny bodies are eight wax glands. When they need to build their waxen honeycomb, they eat honey and hang together in long chains, making a living curtain with their bodies. They produce heat and liquid wax forms in the glands. As it comes into contact with air it solidifies into minute, delicate wafers like fish scales. The bees pick these up with their back legs and transfer them to their front legs, where the wax is held against the jaw. Using their mandibles like a mason's trowel, the bees construct cells which provide cradles for their larvae and storage chambers for their pollen and honey. The resulting comb, melted down and cast into blocks, is the raw material of beeswax polish.

Beeswax melts at 63–65°C

Right: the warm tones and grain patterns of beautiful woods need the right care.

(147–150°F) and so is one of the harder waxes, by far the best for making polish. It gives a soft matt sheen to furniture and floors and has only one slight disadvantage: it makes surfaces a little tacky or sticky and so attracts dust.

To give a more reflective gloss to your polished surface, you will need to add to the beeswax a small amount of another natural wax—a

technique which is also discussed in this chapter. The added wax, called carnauba wax, is a vegetable wax. It helps to make the beeswax polish less tacky.

Beeswax is fairly hard and it will only spread smoothly over a surface if it has been softened. This is done by using a solvent to render it into a more liquid form. The traditional solvent for beeswax is turpentine,

which not only has a pungent, clean smell, but also brings out the delicious aroma of the beeswax. White spirit [mineral spirits] can be a satisfactory substitute for turpentine, but lacks the characteristic scent. You might use a mixture of half turpentine and half spirit. The solvent will evaporate and leave the wax on the wood surface.

Paste polish

You will need:
- A saucepan or similar vessel
- Container to hold hot water
- A hand egg whisk [hand rotary beater] or electric mixer
- A graduated jug marked in millilitres (or pints [fluid ounces])
- Clean, dry, lidded cans, such as tobacco or coffee containers
- 100g (4oz) beeswax (available from chemists [pharmacists], or contact your nearest branch of a Beekeepers' Association)
- 275 ml ($\frac{1}{2}$ pint [10 fl oz]) turpentine or white spirit [mineral spirits]

Shred the beeswax into a vessel standing in hot water. Slowly add the turpentine to cover the beeswax and then stir thoroughly with the hand egg whisk [hand rotary beater] or electric mixer until a paste is formed. You can do this without standing the vessel in hot water; it will just take a little longer to break down the beeswax. Do *not* allow a naked flame near the mixture, since turpentine is highly inflammable and so is its vapour. *Never* warm it over a stove.

Filling the cans: your polish will give more pleasure if it presents an unblemished smooth surface when you open a new container ('real' polish also makes a very acceptable Christmas present.)

Tobacco containers are useful for packing paste polish. Wash the container in hot, soapy water and dry it off in a cool oven. This removes the tobacco smell.

Pour close to the edges of the container to prevent surface bubbles. Try to avoid a draught as folds

and wrinkles may appear on the surface. Do not put on the lid until the polish is cold. Leave the containers undisturbed for several hours.

Emulsion polish
An emulsion is a liquid which contains oily or resinous particles in suspension. Emulsion polish consists of waxes and turpentine (the wax element), suspended in water and soap (the water element).

For the wax element you will need:
- 125 gm ($4\frac{1}{2}$ oz) beeswax
- 550 ml (1 pint [20 fl oz]) turpentine or white spirit [mineral spirits], or a mixture of the two.
- A suitable jar or tin in a pan of water

For the water element you will need:
- 15 gm ($\frac{1}{2}$ oz) pure soap flakes or powder
- 550 ml (1 pint [20 fl oz]) water
- A pan with a pouring lip
- Screw top bottles

Opposite: *beeswax comes in many shades of brown, and many varied textures.*
Right: *screw-top bottles, tins and jars, make good containers for emulsion and wax polishes.*
Below top: *mixing beeswax emulsion polish with the aid of an electric beater.*
Below bottom: *filling bottles with polish.*

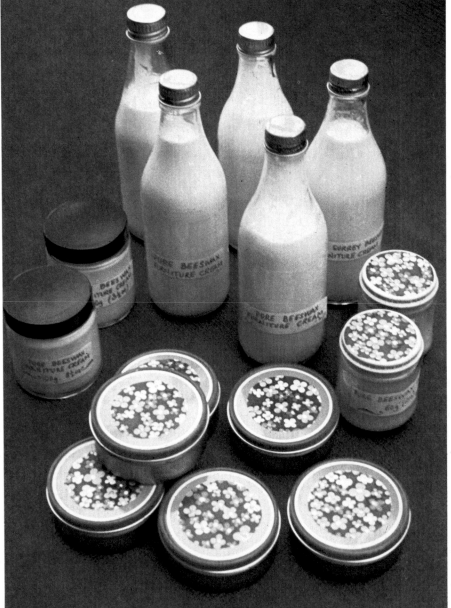

- A funnel
- An electric ring or a gas burner
- A cooking thermometer
- A hand egg whisk [hand rotary beater] or an electric mixer

Melt the wax in a vessel standing in hot water as in the Paste polish recipe. Slowly add the turpentine and/or white spirit [mineral spirits]. Ensure that the pan of hot water is kept at 80°C (180°F). Bring the water to the boil in the pan with the pouring lip, add the soap flakes or powder and heat to 80°C (180°F). The same temperature in the reacting substances produces the best emulsions. Using a hand whisk [hand rotary beater] slowly or an electric mixer at its slowest speed, begin to beat the wax mixture. Very slowly pour the soap and water solution into the wax and continue whisking for several minutes after a good emulsion forms. Pour into clean, warmed bottles (using a funnel to avoid waste).

Carnauba wax

Carnauba wax comes from a palm tree in the Brazilian jungle. To protect its fronds from dehydration in the blazing tropical sun, the carnauba palm covers them with a protective coating of wax. A number of fronds may be cut each year without endangering the tree. They are laid out in rows to dry and turned several times. When the wax begins to flake the fronds are threshed by being beaten with sticks so that the wax falls off.

The carnauba wax flakes are melted over open fires and cast into rough blocks. Carnauba wax, with a melting point of 83–86°C (182–188°F), gives great hardness and gloss to polishes. It has an attractive country scent of newly mown hay.

Carnauba and beeswax polish

The method of making this paste polish is exactly the same as for the pure beeswax paste polish (see p. 48) you simply replace a small amount of beeswax with carnauba wax.

You will need:
- 15 g (½ oz) carnauba wax
- 85 g (3 oz) beeswax
- 550 ml (1 pint [20 fl oz]) solvent (turpentine, white spirit [mineral spirits] or a mixture of the two)

Beeswax and carnauba wax emulsion is exactly the same as that for the beeswax emulsion polish, except that temperatures can be raised to 90°C (195°F) and 25 g (1 oz) of beeswax can be replaced by carnauba wax.

Variations
When you have made a few batches of polish you may wish to experiment and adapt the recipes to your own requirements. If you like a firmer polish, reduce the proportion of solvent in the paste polish. Add extra solvent to emulsion polish and you will have a liquid wax polish, especially suitable for floors. (Note: if adding carnauba wax to floor polish, use only a small amount, or your floor may become dangerously slippery.) If you prefer a high gloss finish on your furniture, increase the proportion of carnauba wax. Do not exceed 30 per cent carnauba in your total wax or you may find that you get too hard a gloss.

Using the polish
Beeswax polish cleans and polishes the surface in one operation. All it needs is energy. Apply a thin coat of polish, allow it to dry thoroughly, then buff to a shine with a dusting cloth. Repeat this process several times rather than trying to build up a thick coating of wax at one go. Remember that thick coatings of wax turn a surface into a dirt trap.

All these polishes are particularly suitable for fine and antique furniture and they are also good for wood block floors or for polishing old fashioned linoleum. They are not suitable, however, for thermoplastic tiled floors and modern articles of furniture which have a synthetic spray finish (many modern finishes should only be wiped clean with a damp cloth). Consult the care tag or your furniture salesman if in doubt.

Warning
Melted wax and wax solvents are flammable substances and should not be heated over a naked flame. Melt wax in a double saucepan or a bowl standing in a pan of water. Watch the whole heating process with care and have a lid ready to smother any flames should the ingredients ignite. Do not attempt to extinguish any flames with water which will only spread the fire. A large damp cloth, sand or a foam fire extinguisher is safer.

Wood polishes
Not all polishes can be used on all types of surface and as there is a bewildering range of polishes now available, it is well worth knowing exactly what each is intended to do.

Some furniture and floor finishes need polishing regularly with preparations that have to be rubbed in well. Others need no polishing at all—only a light spray with a handy aerosol, and a wipe over which cleans the surface as you dust.

Wood polishes for furniture
There are four basic types of furniture polish: wax pastes, liquid waxes, creams and aerosol sprays. Whichever type you use, remember that it is regular applications of polish, sparingly used, that give furniture that lovely rich gleam. Always dust furniture thoroughly before polishing it, to remove any dirt or grit which might scratch the surface. If using a wax paste, warm it slightly to improve absorption.

Apply the polish with a soft lint-free cloth (an old dusting cloth is ideal), rubbing with short, quick strokes across the grain. This fills in any tiny cracks in the surface. Then polish with the grain, using longer strokes. For speed, you can apply the polish to one small area at a time, then polish immediately. If the surface shows a mark after you have pressed a thumb lightly on it, the wax has not been completely absorbed, or you have applied too much. In either case, the rubbing must be continued until the thumb test gives a clear result.

Always keep your polishing cloths clean and store them in plastic bags.

Wax pastes: these are solvent-based and need to be well rubbed in and polished hard to give a good shine. They produce a thin covering layer of hard wax on furniture and are particularly good for surfaces that take a lot of wear, such as table and desk tops. They act as a filler on open-grain wood surfaces like oak, keeping out dirt and building up a smooth, shiny surface. They are rich in wax—blends of natural and synthetic kinds—mixed to make the polish easier to apply. They are best used for any initial application of wax to furniture starved of polish, because of their filling property, although subsequent polishing can be done with the creams which need less effort to apply.

Some wax pastes contain silicones, which give a water-repellent quality and resistance to finger marks. However, it is best not to use these on high quality furniture or antiques where a traditional wood finish has been applied.

Many people with valuable antique furniture like to use beeswax—the traditional wax used in polishes. Pure beeswax polishes are not easy to find, but it is possible to make your own beeswax paste and emulsion (cream) polishes at home (see p. 48).

Liquid wax: this also contains natural and synthetic waxes, but in addition has a solvent that cleans the surface, too. After polishing, a thin protective film of wax remains. It is easier to rub in than paste polish.

Creams: traditional cream polishes contain hard waxes in a water-in-oil emulsion. Most do not contain silicones and are often used on older furniture and antiques where a covering of wax is not wanted, as they give a good shine without polish build-up. They contain more cleaning solvents than liquid wax polishes and are useful for getting rid of sticky fingermarks.

French-polished furniture is best treated with cream polish used very sparingly. Otherwise it is easy to produce a high-gloss surface that is difficult to live with, because it is easily marred by heat and spills and needs constant attention. If French-polished furniture with the subtle gloss the cabinet maker intended is polished too often, it will take on a very high gloss indeed—a look which has gone out of fashion. However, this finish does need cleaning and protecting with a light wax polish occasionally.

Re-polishing a worn waxed surface
First clean off any surface dirt with a cloth lightly dampened with turpentine (*not* white spirit [mineral spirits], which is a turpentine substitute). The turpentine will remove a thin film of the original wax finish. Leave the surface to dry and then rub it over with a cloth before applying fresh wax polish very sparingly. Apply this with circular motions, gradually covering the whole surface, using a dry, lint-free cloth. Polish by rubbing briskly with the grain. To avoid spreading the wax in uneven lumps, it is a good idea to fold the polish between two layers of muslin cloth [cheesecloth].

Oil polishing
If you have stripped a piece of furniture to the original wood, you may prefer to give it a traditional oiled finish rather than a coat of sealer finish. Linseed oil is traditionally used for this. It darkens the colour of the wood, and so is most suitable for mahogany or cherry, giving them a deep rich gleam. It tends to bring out the orange tones in pine, so use olive oil for such woods, simply rubbed on. This finish tends to collect the dirt and rubs off on clothing, so it is not suitable for chairs.

Oiled finishes must only be applied to well-prepared and smoothed surfaces, as any imperfections will show. After a final fine sanding, go over the surface in the

There are silicone creams with a lower wax content, which have silicone oil as their main polishing agent. These are intended for the hard, high-gloss finish found on much modern furniture and give a shine with minimum effort.
Aerosols: these contain a silicone cream polish and the aerosol pack makes it possible to spray the cream on and dust and polish at the same time. Multi-purpose cleaner polishes in aerosol form are also marketed. They contain waxes, emulsifiers, silicones, solvents and other chemicals to preserve the polish and its container. They should only be used on modern hard finishes—a cellulose or polyester lacquer which is sprayed on during manufacture. Cleaner-polishes give a high gloss and only need a light rub. They are also good for use on kitchen units, the outsides of refrigerators, freezers and washing machines, and on windows and mirrors. Cleaner-polish, sprayed on a cloth, will clean venetian blinds and keep curtain tracks running smoothly.

Because these sprays give a water-repellent surface, they help to prevent metal parts of refrigerators and other equipment from rusting. They also help protect garden tools from rust. Do not use them for floors—apart from the expense, they create a slippery surface which could be dangerous.

Other finishes
Modern furniture made of wood with a matt finish, such as teak and afrormosia, should never be polished. Dust regularly and give the occasional rub with teak oil or one of the aerosol liquid sprays specifically designed for these woods. Whatever you use, use it sparingly and seldom.

direction of the grain with very fine steel wool.

Applying the finish: mix five parts of boiled linseed oil with one part of real turpentine. Heat the mixture to simmering point in a jar in a pan of hot water to evaporate any moisture it may contain. Let it cool a little and apply it generously to the surface with a soft cloth. Then rub it well with your hands in the direction of the grain, until the surface no longer feels sticky. Use a series of clean cloths to remove any excess, taking particular care in crevices where it can become sticky or harden. Keep rubbing the wood for about 15 to 20 minutes—the friction helps the mixture to dry.

Leave the wood to dry for at least two days before applying the second coat. After that, apply coats in a similar way, once a week (longer in damp weather), gradually extending the time between each application. Test whether the finish is drying by putting your hand on it for a few minutes. If your hand looks oily, give each coat longer to dry out. Between five and ten coats at least will be needed to produce a burnished gleam. Once this point is reached, the wood can be kept gleaming by a monthly oil application for a year. After this, a once-a-year application will maintain the finish. Do not forget to oil the underside of a table top when oil finishing the top, as a precaution against warping.

Reviving an oil finish: clean the surface with a rag dampened in warm water and soap. When the surface is thoroughly dry apply the oil–turpentine mixture very sparingly. Polish thoroughly with the grain.

Finishing a wood surface

Lovely as it looks, a newly-stripped surface is vulnerable to finger marks, dirt in the air, accidental spills; all tend to sink into the unprotected surface. There are several simple finishing process which will protect the surface without spoiling the natural wood tone or grain.

The simplest finish is traditional shellac. Shellac is a natural resin, sold in various colours from clear to brownish, dissolved in methylated spirits [denatured alcohol]. Thinned to the consistency you like with more methylated spirits [denatured alcohol], it brushes on very easily and smoothly and takes no time to dry. It was the only clear finish used on traditional furniture to about 1850. It dries to a naturally glossy surface, which you can dull down if you like by rubbing with the finest steel wool. It is ideal for sealing coats on top of stained surfaces and for any surface which does not get hard wear. The only problem is that shellac re-dissolves in alcohol and is vulnerable to accidental spills. So it is as well to use it as a finish for vertical surfaces, but not horizontal ones like table tops. Buy a small can for each job, as, once opened, it becomes gummy. To protect a wood surface, dilute the shellac to brushing consistency with a little methylated spirits [denatured alcohol], brush on a coat, allow it to dry, rub well with fine sandpaper (this seals the wood), then give a final coat. For a natural-looking glow, when the final coat has dried, rub the whole piece of furniture with wax polish and the finest steel wool.

Varnished surfaces: modern clear varnishes are plastic-based— polyurethane, melamine or cellulose (the last mostly on pre-war furniture). Any of these types can be found on modern furniture, but only the first is a practical proposition for the home handyman to apply. Polyurethane varnish is easily obtainable and may be clear or tinted, in gloss, satin or matt finishes, and grades suitable for indoor and outdoor use.

How to apply: start with a fresh can of varnish, as it does not keep well. Pour some into a bowl and thin a little with white spirit [mineral spirits] (this helps to prevent bubbles forming as you brush it on); use three tablespoons of spirit to 275 millilitres ($\frac{1}{2}$ pint [10 fl oz]) of varnish. Take a new paintbrush and working against the light (so that you can see if you have missed any area of the surface), apply the varnish evenly and generously, brushing hard. When the surface is covered, holding the brush at an angle of 45°, make long smoothing strokes from one end of the surface to the other. Because the varnish has been thinned, bubble and brush marks will disappear. Let the surface dry thoroughly. The process is most successful if you work in a warm, dust-free room.

A shellac sealing coat, or a coat of thinned varnish, may be applied before the finishing coat. It is important that this coat should be gently rubbed down with the finest steel wool or sandpaper, and the surface carefully dusted between coats. Remember that transparent finishing coats show every flaw in the wood, so preparation work must be scrupulous.

French polishing wood surfaces

French polishing is the name given to a wood finishing process which originated in France during the Middle Ages. By the late seventeenth and eighteenth centuries, French-polished furniture had become fashionable in many European countries and is still unequalled today for its beautiful finish.

French polish is composed mainly of shellac dissolved in methylated spirits [denatured alcohol]. The finish of French-polished furniture is characterized by a smooth and lustrous sheen which accentuates the grain and patterns in the wood. This is the result of the polish technique—a method involving the building up of layers of polish, rather than the ingredients. With patience and experimentation— preferably on a non-precious piece of furniture—you can master the basic skills. Then, with confidence, you can turn an old table or an ageing sideboard in the dining room into attractive pieces of furniture.

Polishes

Nowadays there are numerous liquids available in bottles and sprays which are intended to simulate the appearance of genuine French polishing. These give an easy way out, and if used cleverly, are fairly convincing imitations.

However, it does not take an expert to see that these synthetic substitutes do not give a finish to compare with genuine French polishing. Remember, too, that French polish, being a traditional finish, will not devalue your antique furniture as a more modern finish can.

There are a number of different polishes available for use in French polishing, including transparent, white (for light woods), black (used for ebonizing), garnet (deep brown) and button polish (slightly opaque yellow).

Suitable surfaces
French polish is equally suitable for giving a finish to new furniture or for re-furbishing old articles you may have.

The types of furniture most commonly French polished are table tops, sideboards, chests of drawers et cetera. Dark woods such as mahogany and oak look particularly attractive when given this treat-

ment. But other woods are also suitable, and even whitewood [pine] furniture can be greatly improved in appearance by being French polished. The very shiny finish popular between the World Wars can be softened to a medium sheen which flatters furniture of all periods and is more fashionable these days. French polish is not waterproof, alcohol proof or heat resistant, so bear this in mind when selecting it for your furniture, or be prepared to protect it with cloths, runners and mats.

Re-touching
If an old piece of furniture is already French polished, it is worth considering whether to go as far as stripping off the old surface. Dirty furniture can be sponged with soap and water, dried quickly or cleaned down with a store-bought cleaner. Scratches can be disguised with a little matching oil paint, oil stain or scratch-cover polish. Then when the stain is dry—a day or two

Above: *often a good rub with a damp rag and scouring powder, is all an old French polished piece needs before polishing.*

later—polish with a furniture wax or cream, rubbing hard. Although the surface may not be perfect, you may be able to 'save' a mellowed old piece in this way without having the bother of a complete re-polish. You might also find that only the top of a piece of furniture—which gets the most wear and damage—needs the full re-finishing treatment.

Re-finishing: if, however, the old surface is too far gone for spot treatment, you will need to remove the old finish (see p. 37).

After stripping off the old surface, leave it to dry overnight before carefully sanding down. Always use a fine grade sandpaper or finest steel wool. Never be tempted to use the disc sander with a power tool, as this will scar the wood. Preparation for a surface for polishing—French polish shows

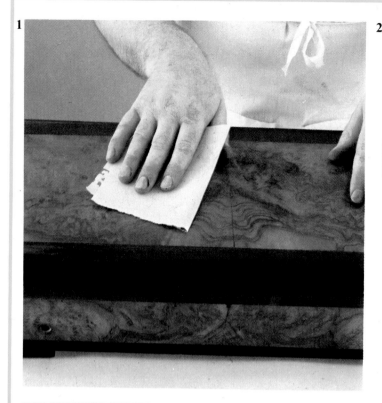

French polishing

1. *Remove the old finish from the piece you intend to polish very carefully. All dust and dirt should be removed by carefully rubbing down the surface with fine sandpaper. Remove any dents which spoil the surface. Any surface faults will show when the re-polishing process is over.*

2. *The next step is to stain the surface if you want to modify the wood colour. Sand the surface scrupulously if the grain has been raised by the stain. Fill the grain if necessary. Let the piece dry, then sand and dust scrupulously as before. Rub on a coat of French polish to seal the surface and sand again.*

3. *French polish should be chosen to suit the wood tone and applied with a polishing pad working swiftly in circles and with the grain. When the first coat is dry, sand the surface carefully. This step seals the prepared wood surface and makes it ready for the final polish build-up.*

4. *At all stages it is essential that every particle of dust be removed before a further coat of polish is applied. A 'tack rag' (that is a cloth kept sticky with varnish) is sometimes used to pick up the dust from freshly sanded surfaces. Keep it ready for use in a screw-topped jar.*

5. *Between coats, as you begin to build up the fine finish, switch to finest steel wool for the sanding process so that the surface is dulled rather than abraded. The durability and glow of the finish depends on the number of coats, each one delicately abraded, which you apply.*

6. *When building up the surface, use a little linseed oil (no more) as a lubricant should the polishing pad show signs of sticking to the surface. The pad must not pause on the surface or your work will be ruined. You will have to learn by experience when to stop applying polish coats.*

7. *Continue swiftly and evenly adding coats of polish until you get the look you want. Store the polishing pad in an airtight jar so it stays soft and pliable. Undo the pad and add some spirit to the cotton wool [absorbent cotton] for the final coats, which should be thin and delicately applied.*

8. *The finished job: you can see how French polish flatters traditional furniture woods like mahogany. The exacting process brings out the beauty of inlaid work and marquetry. You can also dull the finish slightly by a final gentle rub with steel wool and fine wax polish.*

every defect in the surface—must be patiently done by hand, working along the grain, using both hand and eye to check for perfect, silky smoothness. Dust off any dirt and dust scrupulously before you begin the polishing process.

New surfaces: surfaces which have not been previously treated in any way must be made free of dirt and grease. Rub down the wood along the grain, with fine grade sandpaper and wipe away dust and grit.

If you neglect the preparation of your piece of furniture, small faults will become glaring ones as the polishing process progresses and it will be too late to put them right. Therefore, check and double-check that the whole area is smooth, all dents and bruises in the wood removed, scratches sanded out, cracks filled, knots treated with a touch of undiluted shellac.

Grain filling: the surface which has been previously French polished will probably need no grain filling, but new surfaces, especially woods with large pores, such as walnut, mahogany or oak, may need treatment before polishing to get a really smooth surface. Commercial grain fillers in various shades can be bought ready-mixed from hardware stores. Rub the filler well into the grain, wipe clean and dry. If necessary sand with a very fine sandpaper to make the surface perfectly smooth. It is important that the filler be left to dry completely.

Staining: once the surface is smooth, you may wish to alter the wood tone by staining. This is optional and does not affect the actual polishing. Choose a stain which will not raise the grain of the wood—oil stains are the most popular and easiest to use; water and spirit stains can raise the grain so that, when dry, the surface must be carefully sanded yet again. Test out the colour of the stain on a scrap of wood and dilute or deepen it if necessary.

Coating: after filling the grain, staining and sanding, allow the surface to dry, then give a sealing coat of polish, using a polish brush, which works better than an ordinary paint brush. Leave the polish to

dry for at least half an hour, longer if possible. It is best to leave the surface as long as possible between each step in the process so that the filler, stain and polish can set correctly.

Once the polish is dry, sand the surface until it is smooth, using a fine 'flour-grade' sandpaper. Always work with the grain when sanding. Immediately after sanding wipe all dust off the surface with a dry dusting cloth or rag.

Applying the polish: make a French polish applicator [a 'feltpad' which is ideal for French polishing is obtainable from US hardware stores] from a piece of cotton wool [absorbent cotton] 15 cm (6 in) square, folded in half to make a triangle, the corners of which are then folded in to make a pear shape. Cut a piece of lint-free cotton (old sheet or handkerchief) about 18 cm (7 in) square. Soak it in methylated spirits [denatured alcohol] and wring out. Put the cotton wool [absorbent cotton] in the middle of the rag and pour on enough shellac or French polish so it is soaked through but not dripping. Wrap the rag round the cotton wool [absorbent cotton], twisting the edges at the back, flattening the pad and making sure there are no creases on the front of the pad. Press the pad on a piece of wood so that the polish oozes through. By twisting the rag at the back you can control the flow of polish. The pad should fit comfortably into the palm of the hand and looks like half a pear. It is very important to put the right amount of polish on the pad, as too much will cause ridges and blobs, which you cannot remove except by taking all the surface off (with methylated spirits [denatured alcohol]) and starting again. For the same reason, do not press too hard on the surface when the pad is freshly full of polish.

Rub the polish-soaked pad on to the surface, first rubbing across the grain (this helps to fill it) in long strokes from edge to edge, neither pausing anywhere on the surface or going over any area twice. Let the first coat dry for about 20 minutes,

then sand it down carefully, dust off and repeat the process, until, by looking at the surface against the light, you can see that it is evenly covered and the grain filled. Leave the work overnight, with the polishing pad kept in a screw-topped jar. This step gives the basic coat of finish to the surface.

Build up the coats of polish. Starting in one corner of the surface, rub the pad in little circles across to the other side, then back again, overlapping the circles until the whole surface is covered. Undo the pad when dry and pour a little more polish on to the pad. As the amount of polish in the pad decreases, your pressure on the surface must increase to ensure that the pad is dried out before it is re-charged with polish. As before, do not pause or go back over your work, but glide the pad on and off the edges. The polish dries in minutes and after a few coats you will see the surface building up. Should the pad feel a little sticky, smear a fingerful of linseed oil on it for lubrication. If in doubt—stop, as it is better to have a thin perfect surface than to mar the work at this point.

When you are satisfied with the look of the surface—this is where experience comes in—undo the pad and pour some methylated spirits [denatured alcohol] on the back of the pad. Re-twist the pad and apply it in long smooth strokes along the grain from one side of the surface to the other. Again, never pause or go back on your work. Let the work dry overnight. If you prefer a satin finish, the gloss can be softened with finest sandpaper or steel wool, and a little furniture polish for lubrication.

Remember that, at any stage, the surface can be removed by rubbing with methylated spirits [denatured alcohol], and the process started again. One of the things experience teaches is to avoid the careless movement of the pad which can spoil the look of all your previous patient work. Once you get the feel of the technique, it is a fast process. A professional could re-finish a table top in a morning.

Perfect
Veneering

The price of wood gets higher every year, particularly the price of expensive and decorative hardwoods. As a result, more and more pieces of furniture that would once have been made of solid mahogany or teak are now built from a less expensive softwood or chipboard and covered with a decorative hardwood veneer, giving much the same effect as solid wood. Some decorative woods are too fragile or unstable to use in solid form, and these, too, are applied as veneers. Veneered furniture is easily damaged. Cigarette burns, knocks from family rough and tumble, loose pieces of veneer catching on clothing and tearing, all can damage an impeccable surface. If furniture decorated with pieces of veneer or marquetry is kept in damp or over-heated places, the veneered areas can lift and bubble.

You can apply or patch veneered surfaces by hand without too much specialized equipment. But try to avoid anything except flat surfaces to begin with. If curves must be veneered, you can achieve reasonable, though not first-class, results by sticking a patch on with contact adhesive. And there are various tricks that will help you disguise the join between the old and new areas.

Buying and handling veneer

Finding the veneer you want for a particular job is not easy, and you may need to take time and trouble. The ideal place, of course, is a specialist veneer and marquetry dealer, but there are few of them even in large cities. They generally insist that you buy a whole sheet of veneer at a time. There is no standard sheet size—it varies with suppliers. Antique dealers who do their own restoration possibly have, and might sell, a small piece of veneer to you. Larger art and handicraft shops sell small pieces of veneer for the craft of marquetry. There are also firms which sell small pieces of veneer by mail order.

Nearly all veneer is the same thickness. An exception to this is the veneer border round the leather top of some desks and tables. Here, the veneer has to be the same thickness as the leather, and must be specially ordered. To replace missing bits of marquetry, you may have to build up the piece of veneer, or gently sand it down, once in place, to match up with the surrounding wood. If you cannot buy a veneer to match the wood you need, buy a lighter piece. You can always darken it to match. Re-

member that the polishing process darkens the wood in any case. To test this, dampen a corner of the veneer you are using. This will give you some idea of the tone it will be when finished. Always handle veneer carefully, particularly in large sheets. It splits very easily.

Methods of veneering

Veneer can be adhered with Scotch glue [hot pure hide] – the traditional glue used for wood working), pva [polyvinyl acetate glue] adhesive, contact adhesive. Because of the differences between these adhesives, the method of applying the veneer differs in each case. Use Scotch or hide glue for older furniture; if pva [polyvinyl acetate] and Scotch glue are used side by side the pva [polyvinyl acetate] will not stick. Scotch glue is solid when cold and only becomes liquid and adhesive when heated. As it cools, it soon becomes too thick to flow easily, so it must be kept hot while in use. In contrast, pva [polyvinyl acetate] adhesive is a water-based glue which flows easily at all times and in normal conditions takes many hours to set. Contact or instant bonding adhesive makes both surfaces stick fast on contact, but does not hold as strongly as the others.

Opposite: *the right veneer gives a precious look to a wooden box.*
Right: *here is an elegant piece of furniture in need of repair. Note the damaged edge where the veneered surface must be matched and replaced.*

The Scotch glue method

The principle of the traditional Scotch glue method, correctly called 'hammer veneering', is to spread hot, liquid Scotch glue on both surfaces, lay the veneer in place and work excess glue out from underneath the veneer by rubbing (not banging, or the wood will be damaged) with a special veneer hammer which features an excellent smoothing edge. This gives a smooth, flat finish. It is important to use the veneer hammer, otherwise the glue may give a rippled surface. If the glue dries before the work is completed, it can be re-heated by ironing the surface of the veneer with a heavy iron. The glue holds the veneer firmly in place from the moment it is applied, but takes about two weeks to finish setting and gain its full strength. Apart from its use in the repair of traditional furniture, the Scotch glue method is best for covering large areas—say 60 cm (24 in) square and above.

Removing old veneer: Scotch glue softens when wetted. Lay hot, wet rags over the surface and apply a hot iron to make the water boil. Continue as the veneer begins to peel. When it does, take an old carving knife or chisel and work it under the edges to lever the veneer off. Scrape any traces of softened glue from the core wood and finish with methylated spirits [denatured alcohol].

You will need:

- Sufficient Scotch glue (it may be available in a solid sheet, or small balls known as pearls, or in a semi-liquid state)
- A glue pot: improvise this by using two cans, one of a size to fit inside the other with 25 mm (1 in) space all round it. Fill the larger pot with a few inches of water and drop a few bolts or stones into the bottom. Put the

Scotch glue in the smaller can and place it in the larger one on top of the bolts. This allows the glue to be heated without any risk of burning
- A heat source. Any type of stove will do
- A veneer plane [toothing plane] to roughen a new surface to be veneered or coarse sandpaper wrapped around a block will be just as suitable
- A veneer hammer
- A sharp knife, a sharp chisel and a metal rule
- A clean rag and hot water

- Various grades of sandpaper down to 'flour' (the very finest) grade
- Roll of brown paper tape
- Wood filler

Remove the old veneer, or if veneering a piece for the first time, roughen it with a veneer or toothing plane or coarse sandpaper, both used at an angle of 45° to the grain, to give a good key for the glue. If the surface is particularly absorbent, as in the case of very coarse-grained wood, give it a coat of Scotch glue thinned with water.

This will prevent so much glue being absorbed that the veneer does not stick properly. Now examine and match the pieces of veneer to give the most attractive grain pattern. Using the knife and metal rule, cut the veneer into pieces about 25 mm (1 in) oversize round the edge of the surface to be covered. If two or more pieces are being laid next to each other, lay them in place with the edges overlapping by an inch. Then cut through the centre of the line of the overlap along a steel rule, cutting through both pieces at once. Be sure to hold the knife vertical. Discard the scraps and stick the pieces edge to edge with ordinary brown paper tape or veneer tape.

Heat the Scotch glue until it melts and add a little water to keep it thin. Dampen the veneer on both sides. Spread the glue evenly but as thinly as possible over the wood surface and the back of the veneer. Work quickly as the glue soon thickens. Lay the first sheet in place. Take the veneering hammer and draw it over the veneer along the grain but with the blade slanted at an angle of about 45° to the grain. Always use a scraping movement with the veneer hammer, never a tapping one, as this could mark the surface. Try to keep an even pressure on the hammer at all times. Clean off any glue that oozes out round the edges with a hot, wet cloth.

The Scotch glue may set before the veneer has been pressed completely smooth, but you can soften the glue so that it can be worked again by ironing it with a warm iron.

Always keep the surface slightly damp to allow the veneer hammer to slip easily over it and to prevent the veneer from being scorched by the iron. But try not to re-heat the glue more than necessary, as you may dry out the veneer and cause contraction cracks.

When you have smoothed over the whole piece, check the surface for bubbles or ripples. Go over the whole area carefully, tapping it with your fingernails. If it sounds hollow anywhere, there is an air bubble underneath. If the surface is uneven but does not sound hollow, there is a lump of glue under it. To remove these faults, iron that area and slit the surface in the direction of the grain with a razor blade or modelling knife. Work over the area with the veneer hammer to squeeze out any air or excess glue. Then stick a piece of brown paper over the cut. This prevents it from opening up and air being drawn back beneath the veneer. For the same reason stick brown paper around all the edges of the sheet of veneer.

Leave the veneer to dry for two weeks. Then trim the edges with the knife, being careful not to damage the surface. If the veneer overlaps a corner, use a chisel to trim it to size. Dampen and remove any brown paper stuck to the surface. Rub the whole surface lightly along the grain with fine sandpaper, followed by flour-grade paper [emery cloth]. Spread colour-matched wood filler, such as Brummer stopping, mixed with methylated spirits [denatured alcohol], over the whole surface to seal the grain and hide the joins, and rub down again. If you are re-veneering part of an old piece of furniture, stain the new veneer to match the old, using the scraps to test the colour. French polish the surface.

The pva [polyvinyl acetate] and G [C]-clamp method

This is best for small areas and when using curly, wavy or burr veneers, which are hard to lay flat. The base wood and the back of the veneer are both coated with pva [polyvinyl acetate] adhesive. The veneer is put in position and a piece of wood clamped in place on top of the veneer. The piece of wood should be the same size, or the veneer will curl. Since this type of glue flows easily, the excess will be forced out by the pressure of the clamps, and as long as the clamped down wood surface, whatever its size, is really flat, the veneer will have a perfectly smooth surface. The clamps are essential to prevent the veneer lifting during the 15 or so hours the adhesive takes to dry; they must be arranged so as to exert an equal pressure all over the board. The greatest width that can be tackled adequately is about 60 cm (24 in). You can veneer long strips of this width by using several clamps.

You will need:
- pva [polyvinyl acetate] adhesive
- A mixing pot
- A sharp handyman's knife
- Chisel
- Sandpaper in various grades
- Large sheet of brown paper (if needed)
- Pieces of wood, or large flat, thick, smooth board, big enough to cover the veneered area
- G [C]-clamps

Remove the existing veneer and clean the wood surface with sandpaper, but do not roughen it. Match the veneers and cut them oversize, but do not wet them. If you are laying two pieces side by side, do not overlap them. Cut the adjacent edges along a steel rule so that they can be butted accurately against each other.

Water down the pva [polyvinyl acetate] glue—one part water to five parts glue. Spread it evenly over the surfaces to be joined—keeping it off the top of the veneer—and place the veneer in position. The adhesive is very fluid so that the clamps will press any excess adhesive out at the sides of the sheets. A veneering hammer is not, therefore, necessary.

Lay the sheet of brown paper (if needed) over the veneer and put the flat board on top of it. Clamp the board in place with at least one clamp every 60 cm (24 in). The brown paper prevents the veneer from sticking to the board. Tighten the central clamps first, then the outer ones, so as not to create a bubble. Leave to dry for about 24 hours, then remove the clamps and board. Trim the veneer, sand and finish as before.

The pva [polyvinyl acetate] and steam iron method

The veneer is stuck to the wood base with pva [polyvinyl acetate] adhesive as before, but no clamps are used to hold the veneer in place. Instead the veneer is ironed in place with an electric steam iron for a few minutes. This both forces out any excess adhesive and speeds up the drying time, so that the veneer stays in place and the whole job is dry in a couple of hours. But it is very easy, by careless ironing, to leave a lump of glue under the surface of the veneer. This lump cannot be ironed out later, as with the Scotch glue method, for heat causes the pva [polyvinyl acetate] adhesive to harden. In practice, only small areas are ever veneered in this way. It is a useful method for making veneer patches in modern furniture.

You will need:
- pva [polyvinyl acetate] adhesive
- Mixing pot
- Handyman's knife and steel rule
- Chisel
- Sandpaper
- Clean rag
- Steam iron set to 50°C (120°F)

Prepare the surface, cut the veneer and glue it on as in the previous method. Then iron the veneer: any indentations caused by centre of each piece of veneer and working to the edges. Never stop moving the iron, and try to apply even pressure all over so that you finish with a smooth surface to the veneer: any indentations caused by the iron will be plainly visible. Keep the surface moist, so that the veneer is not scorched. The adhesive will dry in a few minutes—you should be able to feel when this happens. Once it has dried, nothing can be done to iron out bubbles or lumps: unlike Scotch glue, the adhesive cannot be softened.

Contact adhesive
This is too thick for normal use, and not very strong. It should only be used as a last resort when all other methods are impossible. Simply spread both surfaces as thinly and evenly as possible with adhesive, leave it for the time recommended by the manufacturer to become tacky (usually 10 minutes) and press it into place. A

veneer hammer is useful for pressing it down, but you cannot use it for removing lumps of glue under the veneer. If there are any lumps, they will have to stay. Air bubbles can be removed by the method previously described.

Modern thixotropic contact adhesive gives you a few seconds to slide the veneer into the right position before you press it permanently into place. If you have to use this method at all, buy this kind of adhesive, not the sort that gives an instant bond.

Other methods
A special plastic 'glue film' can be bought in sheets. This is laid under the veneer, which should be moistened on the top surface only, and the film is melted through the veneer with a cool electric iron, not a steam iron. A veneer hammer is used on the softened film exactly as with Scotch glue, though you may find that less smoothing will be necessary.

The method is simple and effective, and reasonably economical. It should not, however, be used for veneering surfaces that are going to be subjected to heat, for example, shelving over radiators. *To sum up:* use the Scotch glue method when covering large areas or repairing pieces previously veneered with Scotch glue. For small areas and modern furniture, use the pva [polyvinyl acetate] and G [C]-clamp method, when it is possible to apply G [C]-clamps. Where this is not possible, use the pva [polyvinyl acetate] and steam iron method. Try not to use contact adhesive, except as a last resort.

Starting to use veneer
Edge and back treatment
When two surfaces at right angles to each other—such as the edge and top of a table top—are being veneered, one piece of veneer must overlap the other. This join will later be filled and sanded smooth, so it will not be very obvious. But you should make sure that the surface that is seen most, overlaps the surface that is seen least—for example, the veneer on the top of a

table should overlap that on the edge. In this case, veneer the edges first, allowing the veneer to overlap both sides of the edges. Leave the glue to dry for two days then trim the pieces to size so that the top edge is exactly smooth and level with the table top. Then veneer the top of the table and leave it for two weeks to dry before finishing.

An attractive method of finishing the edges of a table is to fix strips of solid wood matching the veneer to the edges with glue and the very thin panel pins [finishing nails] which are called veneer pins. This method gives a more robust result, since the edges of a veneered table are most easily damaged. But the top veneer must not overlap the edging strip, or the different rate of expansion of table and edging will split it. If veneer is applied to one side only of a board, it will create considerable stress on that side, causing the wood to warp or bow. To prevent this, cover the other side with a veneer of equal thickness. For economy, a less expensive veneer can be used for the backing if it is not seen.

Patching veneer
Most damage to veneered furniture is to the edge of a top surface, but fortunately this is also the easiest part to repair invisibly.

Whenever possible, repair a damaged edge by removing and replacing a straight strip running along the whole edge of the piece with the grain of the existing veneer. In this way the old and new pieces will be joined along the line of their grain, thus concealing the join. The join will also be a straight line which makes it easier to fit.

First remove the polish around the damaged area with a cabinet scraper or molding chisel in order to discover the natural colour of the wood. Match a piece of new veneer to the old wood. A quick way of seeing whether the new piece will match when polished is to wet it; this shows what it will look like when polished. Wet both sides of the veneer to prevent warping.

Using the chisel, remove the damaged area of veneer. Hold the

The veneer on this antique box lid was badly damaged along one edge, and a strip needed replacing completely.

1. Gently remove the polish around the damaged area with a cabinet scraper.

2. It is important to match the new veneer to the area from which the polish has been removed. Dampen a tiny area of the new veneer, on both sides, to see how it will look when the finishing coat is applied.

3. It is possible to deepen the tone of new veneer, but not to lighten it.

4. Gently remove the damaged strip of old veneer, holding the chisel bevel side up at the edge.

5. Use the chisel bevel side down for the rest of the damaged veneer.

6. Dampen delicate veneers on both sides before cutting. Use a sharp craft or handyman's knife and a heavy straight edge to avoid splitting the wafer-thin veneer.

7. The edges of a piece of furniture take hard wear, so choose the adhesive with care. Traditionally, Scotch glue (an animal glue) is used.

8. Hold the piece of veneer in place to ensure accurate grain matching and cut carefully to fit.

9. When all pieces of veneer are set in place, force out extra glue and air bubbles by rubbing with a Warrington or veneer hammer. Clamp the patch with G[C]-clamps, protecting the surface with blocks of wood or thin metal plates.

10. If you use pva [polyvinyl acetate] glue, you can iron the veneer in place. The heavier the iron, the better.

11. A short, straight-grained patch in an edge (like the chair here) should be cut larger in a wedge shape and gently pressed in sideways to hold it firmly. Trim the ends to fit with a very sharp chisel or handyman's knife.

12. Veneers with a curly or knotty grain pattern should be joined along the lines of the grain for an unobtrusive patch.

chisel bevel side up at the edge, and bevel side down further in to act as a lever. Cut the new veneer to fit, using a rule and trimming knife. Delicate veneers should be dampened on both sides before cutting as this helps prevent splitting.

Use Scotch glue to stick the new veneer in place, using the method described on p. 59. Once the glue has set, the new veneer can be trimmed on the outer edges with a very sharp chisel or trimming knife.

This method is only suitable for veneer with a fairly straight grain. Knotty veneer, veneer damaged at the end of the line of the grain, or in the middle of a surface, is better repaired by the following method.

It is possible to replace an area of damaged veneer with a boat-shaped patch—that is, an oval shape with pointed ends. The oval points longways along the general direction of the grain, which makes it less obvious when glued down and subtly blends it into the overall surface grain. The more a join runs across the grain, the more it will show, so the ends of the oval should be as pointed as possible. Find out the best shape and size for the patch by putting a piece of tracing paper over the damaged area and drawing boat shapes on it until you find one which looks right. Draw a few lines along it to show the direction of the grain.

Use a piece of carbon paper to transfer the shape to the new veneer. Press very lightly and make sure the grain is running the right way by referring to the lines on the tracing.

Cutting the patch: with a very sharp handyman's knife (complete with new blade) cut out the patch. Slope the knife sideways as you cut, so that the cut edge is on a slant; the handle of the blade should point outwards at an angle of 45°. It is a good idea to cut out the shape slightly too large, as this gives you a chance to move it around over the damaged area to match the grain more exactly. When cutting a straight strip of veneer it is not necessary to slope the knife. Take the oval cut-out and lay it over the damaged area. Move it until the

grain is a good match, then hold it in place and draw around it lightly with a sharp pencil. Now remove the patch and cut around the mark, just inside the pencil line, holding the knife at the same 45° angle as you used for cutting out the patch. Be sure to cut out as little as possible of the old veneer; if the patch proves too big you can trim it down, but if it is too small you will have to cut a new patch. The slanting join, however, helps to hide any small discrepancies.

Remove the damaged veneer inside the cut line with a very sharp narrow chisel, held bevel side down. Be careful to chisel out just the old veneer and the glue under it, without damaging the wood to which the veneer is glued. Keep your chisel sharp. Remove large areas of old glue with a rag and hot water, but be careful not to soften the glue holding the undamaged veneer.

Try the patch in the hole and trim it to size if necessary.

Glueing in the patch: patches in veneer need to be glued very strongly and held in place while the glue dries. Choose the right kind of glue: pva [polyvinyl acetate] for modern furniture, Scotch glue for old furniture. Use the Scotch glue method as outlined on p. 59, but clamp the patch in place with a G [C]-clamp and a wood block, the size of the patch under it, and a piece of brown paper to absorb any surplus glue which might ooze out. Improvise a clamp with, say, a sheet of glass and three or four bricks carefully laid on top of it.

A patch glued with pva [polyvinyl acetate] adhesive may be ironed in place as described in the method on p. 60.

Finishing the patch: when the glue is thoroughly dry (do not try to rush this), pull off as much of the brown paper as will come off—dampening the paper very carefully helps. Then wrap some very fine sandpaper round a wood block and sand off all traces of paper and glue, until the surface of the patch is level with the veneer around it. Obviously, this will remove some of the finish from the old veneer surrounding

the patch. Sand along the grain when at all possible. Finish the sanding with flour-grade or very fine paper for a smooth surface.

If the surface is very light coloured, or the veneer has a coarse open grain (woods such as oak, ash, rosewood, sapele), seal the surface with a grain filler in a matching colour. This prevents the polish sinking into the wood, discolouring it and making it hard to work up a good finish. Rub the filler into the veneer, and when dry, sand it smooth with flour-grade or very fine paper.

Making the patch match: before applying any French polish to the patch, make sure that it will turn the right colour when polished. Ordinary uncoloured French polish darkens wood only slightly. Examine the area around the patch where the old polish has been sanded off. If it is not exactly the same colour as the patch itself, you will need to stain the patch to match. You can test this by applying several coats to a scrap of the patch veneer. To stain the patch, use a ready-mixed, spirit-based wood stain. Choose the right tone—reddish, yellowish, or whatever. You can always dilute the polish with methylated spirits [denatured alcohol] to make it paler. Experiment on scraps to get the right colour, then paint the patch. A water-based wood dye is not suitable because it is hard to control the spread of the colouring.

When the colour is right and dry, finish with French polish. Some modern furniture has a satin finish. Duplicate this by painting the veneer with a 50/50 mixture of clear polyurethane varnish and white spirit [mineral spirits], rubbing when dry with a very fine steel wool and a little oil or polish. Do not use modern finishes on valuable old furniture; stick to the traditional shellac and French polish finishes which can always be removed, renovated and repaired without harming the wood.

Opposite: *marquetry can be both handsome and useful, as shown in this carefully restored chessboard.*

Repairing Rush, Cane and Seagrass Chairs

Cane

Caned chair seating dates back to ancient Egypt and although nothing was written about the technique until this century, early artefacts, such as Tutankhamun's day-bed, show that the method has changed very little.

Caned furniture has been fashionable over the centuries, but especially during the past 300 years. In the eighteenth century finer cane than was previously used became available in Europe, and elegant cane-bottomed chairs made by cabinet-makers, such as Adam and Hepplewhite, were the result.

Caning reached its greatest popularity in the nineteenth century with the development of bentwood furniture, and in Vienna one factory produced 400,000 bentwood chairs in a year. Bentwood pieces are popular again and furniture which needs re-caning can often be bought at a reasonable price. It is a craft worth pursuing; it is not difficult—it merely requires a methodical approach, and there can be few crafts which require fewer tools. Most of these are part of a household's regular equipment or can be improvised.

Do not be too ambitious in the early stages, however. Leave antique chairs alone until you become experienced at handling and weaving cane. Start with a simple square or oblong shape before attempting more complicated ones. Very large articles should not be tackled for your first attempt, as not only are these harder to do, but will take so long at a beginner's slow pace that you will probably get bored and give up. Later, when you have the skills, you will be able to cover large areas quite quickly.

Chair seating cane or reed comes from a vine which grows in South-East Asia. It is a member of the rattan family and grows to enormous lengths. The outer bark has sharp barbs, but this is discarded. Underneath is a hard, shiny inner bark and this is used for caning chairs.

Right: a classic caned chair seat.

The cane comes in two qualities and six sizes. Blue tie (first quality) is the best cane and is used for antique chairs, but red tie (flat reed) is suitable for most other chairs. The sizes are numbered from one to six. The thinner the cane the smaller the number. Two different sizes of cane are often used on one chair: the most commonly used sizes are two and six.

The size of cane required depends on the distance between the holes on the chair frame. The usual distance between holes is 13 mm ($\frac{1}{2}$ in), making the frame suitable for the ever-popular seven-step pattern. If the holes in a frame are closer together than 13 mm ($\frac{1}{2}$ in), the cane will become crowded, making it difficult to work, and size two or three must be used instead. For very fine work, use sizes one and two. Very fine cane is usually used for finishing off the chair seat. If you are re-caning a chair, take a sample if possible, and buy a similar size.

Cane or reed can be bought in craft or hobby shops and from some specialist mail order craft suppliers. A bundle of cane will be more than sufficient for one chair (your supplier will advise you the correct size of bundle); working with different sizes may mean left-over material unless you plan to repair several chairs.

You will need:

- **Pegs:** These are used to hold the cane temporarily during the weaving, although some are left permanently to secure odd ends or to plug 'blind' holes. Any fine pointed sticks, such as tooth-picks or cocktail sticks, are suitable, as is thick basket cane, if you have it. Alternatively, for temporary pegs you can use golf tees
- **Scissors.** Any size will do as long as they make a clean cut
- **Knife** to cut the cane where scissors cannot reach. It can also be used to make and shape the pegs
- **Hole clearer:** A 75mm (3in) nail is suitable if the pointed end is cut or filed off. Similarly, a metal knitting needle or awl, gimlet or screwdriver can be used. The diameter of the tool should not be more than 3mm ($\frac{1}{8}$in)
- **Bodkin:** A small fine bodkin is very useful to help the cane through tight spaces, but you can make do with a hat pin or a large rug needle
- **Small hammer** for rapping the knots flat at the finish and for tapping the pegs into holes

Preparation

First strip off all the old cane and pull out any small nails or wooden pegs that have been used to secure pieces of cane into the holes. Discard these. The old cane can be cut away close to the frame and kept for reference—this is especially useful if the shape is irregular. Before removing the old cane make a sketch of the frame, marking the holes and the number of canes from each hole and their direction—this is useful when

caning round and oval shapes. Use the clearer to knock all the pegs out of the holes. If a gentle tap will not do, it is less strain on the chair frame if you drill a hole in the peg, using a drill bit the same size as the hole. Sometimes corner holes are 'blind'—that is, they do not go right through the wood. Here the pegs must be drilled out to clear the original hole. Any repairs or renovations to the frame must be done before caning starts. Sand and re-varnish the chair at this stage, if necessary, as this is not possible once the weaving has started.

The cane must be prepared before use. Soak the bundle of cane in hot water until it becomes easy to handle. Although dry cane is very brittle and cracks easily, do not keep the cane soaking or you will discolour it, and do not wrap it in a damp cloth or keep it in a plastic bag. Dip each piece in water just before using it, and keep it moist enough to use by dipping your fingers in a bowl of water and stroking the non-glossy side of the cane from time to time. Be careful not to step on the cane, as it can split and the split can then run the length of the reed. Discard split pieces: they spoil the look of the work.

Step One: put tees in the centre holes at front and back of the chair seat. Put a tee in the left hand back hole next to the back left corner hole. Count the number of holes between the two back tees. Count the same number to the left of the front centre tee and mark with a fourth tee. This will keep the cane lines straight. Take out the tee in the back left corner, insert one end of the cane, allowing a 10cm (4in) tail to protrude underneath the frame, keeping the glossy surface facing upwards. Peg the cane firmly in the hole. Take the long end of the cane across and through the hole marked with a tee on the front edge of the frame. Make sure that the glossy side of the cane is upwards and there are no twists. Make sure the cane is not twisted as it goes through the hole. Pull it fairly tight and peg it. The cane is now brought up through the next hole, un-

twisted, glossy side always up—even on the underside of the frame. Pull tight and secure with another peg or tee. The cane is now passed to the back frame to the hole next to the starting one. Take another peg, or remove the second peg to peg the cane in this hole. The first peg holds the cane end, but each successive peg can be taken from a hole to 'travel' with the weaving. Keep the cane taut but not too tight, as it shrinks as it dries. Continue going backwards and forwards until you reach the centre pegs, then mark the right side holes with pegs as before and continue until the other side is reached.

If the cane runs out, leave the end protruding from the underside and leave a peg in the hole to hold the cane securely until the ends are finished off. Then start a new length of cane in the next hole just as you started the first piece of cane. Always leave 10cm (4in) protruding from the underside, for old and new lengths of cane. Fill in the sides of the seat with separate cane strands, keeping the cane at the sides parallel to that fitted already but do not use any of the four corner holes. Secure loose ends with extra tees. You will need to do this if your seat is wider at the front than at the back. Take the cane from the front hole next to the one you have already filled and back to the most convenient hole on the side of the chair that will keep the strand of cane exactly parallel to the previous one. This may be the side hole next to the corner hole, or it may not, according to the shape of the seat. The important thing is to keep the strands parallel and to keep the work the same on both sides of the chair. Use up all the front holes until you reach the corner hole.

Step Two: string the frame from side to side. There are usually the same number of holes in both sides, so you can start at the front and work to the back without interruption. Lay the cane *over* the Step One caning at right angles.

Opposite: *patience and perseverance makes a successful caned seat like this.*

Step Three: repeat Step One *on top* of the previous two steps. Make the next step easier by positioning Step Three cane so that it does not lie directly on top of Step One canes but parallel to it. Keep to the right of the first step, especially at the holes. Tying in the ends: you can tie in the loose ends, if you wish, as you work. Pass the new end untwisted twice over the short strands between holes on the underside of the chair.

Step Four: this is a repetition of Step Two but, unlike Step Two, the cane must be woven *under* then *over,* the vertical caning (not over and under). This step takes longer than any other step. Run your fingers along a length of cane in both directions, and then use the cane in the direction which feels smoother. This helps the cane to slip more easily in and out of the other strands. Start as for Step Two and peg one end.

The cane must be kept untwisted and the right way up. Starting from the fixed end, run the cane through your fingers, keeping it untwisted all the way to the working end. This is very important as there is no way of untwisting it once woven unless you undo the work. Having untwisted the cane, thread the end underneath the cane of Step One (the one on the left), up between the two vertical canes and over Step Three.

Repeat with each pair of canes as you reach them. Do not pull the whole length of cane through until you have passed six pairs. As you pull the cane through it will flatten, straighten and tighten the work. Continue back and forth, joining in cane as required and pegging protruding ends. Keep the pattern correct. Remember that in this step the cane goes *under* the Step One caning and *over* Step Three. Do not worry too much about making the lines neat and tidy with close, even little squares—the next two steps will do this.

Step Five: the first diagonal. If you have been using thin cane, now is the time to change to the next size. Otherwise continue with same size cane. Peg the cane end in the back

left hand corner. Start weaving over the first pair of horizontals (Steps Two and Four) move over to the right, by going *under* the next vertical pair (Steps One and Three) then *over* the next horizontal pair, and so on. The weaving feels as it is done in 'steps' but once it is pulled through tightly it forms a diagonal.

If the chair frame is square, you will end in the opposite corner, otherwise thread it into whichever hole you reach. Bring the cane (untwisted) up through the next hole in the front frame to the left and weave back. Keep the pattern correct—over the horizontals and under the verticals. Weave like this until you complete one corner passing straight across from one hole to the other. Go back to the starting hole and start another cane (the corner holes are used twice) to fill the rest of the first diagonals. Go under the verticals, over horizontals as before. Complete the weaving then check to make sure that the pattern is correct. Remember that the only way to correct errors is to unpick the work. The weaving is usually easy and does not need tugging and pulling. If you have any trouble, check again that the pattern is correct.

Step Six: the second diagonal. This is exactly the opposite to Step Five. Start in another corner and weave at right angles to the previous diagonals. Corner holes are used twice again. But this time the cane goes *under* the horizontals and *over* the verticals.

Finishing ends: by now the frame will have quite a number of pegs holding various ends of cane. These can now be tied as previously described, if you have not done so already. Dampen the ends to make them pliable. Cut each end to a point. Thread the end twice under the loop next to it, using the bodkin if necessary to ease the cane gently into position. Keep the ends untwisted, glossy side outwards. Tap the 'coil' gently with the hammer to flatten it and cut the end off close. If you have three or four ends coming out of the same hole, tying-in can be awkward. Pass the cane to be tied under an adjacent

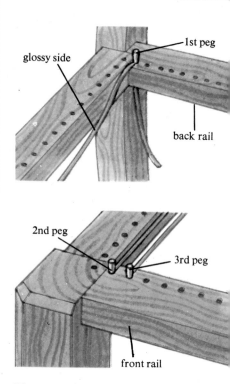

First steps in pegging
Top: *peg the end of the cane to start the first step.*
Above : *cane is temporarily pegged in place here.*

Caning step-by-step (opposite page)
1. *Starting off the vertical caning.*
2. *Lay the cane horizontally* over *the vertical caning.*
3a and 3b. *Further vertical caning parallel to Step 1.*
4. *Caning placed horizontally, but woven* under *then* over *the vertical caning.*
5. *The first diagonal step of the pattern.*
6. *The second diagonal step of the pattern.*
7. *Tying in of loose ends of cane can be done as you work. Pass the new end, untwisted, twice over the short strands on the underside of the seat between holes.*
8. *Beading or molding is the final (optional) step. A line of cane is laid around the outline of the weaving to hide the holes and is couched down with thinner twine.*
9. *Here is a top and sectional view of the finishing process.*

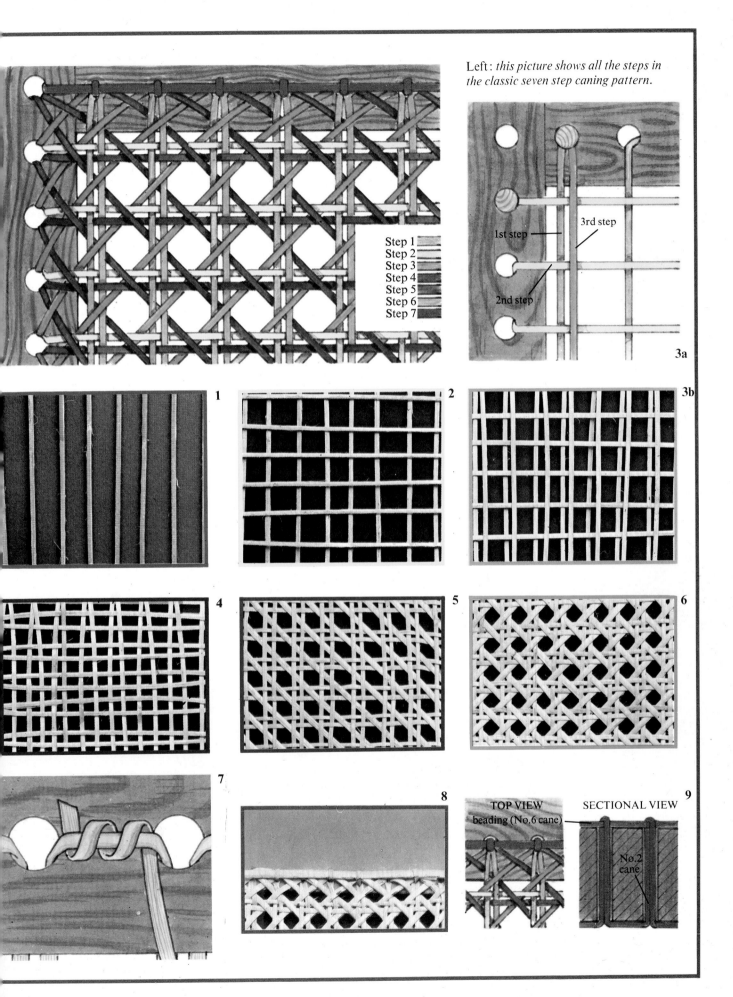

Left: *this picture shows all the steps in the classic seven step caning pattern.*

Step 1
Step 2
Step 3
Step 4
Step 5
Step 6
Step 7

3rd step

1st step

2nd step

3a

3b

1

2

4

5

6

7

8

TOP VIEW
beading (No.6 cane)

SECTIONAL VIEW

No.2
cane

9

loop then take it back under itself and cut off the end.

Permanent pegs are used in blind corners and in holes which hold loose ends which cannot be tied in position. The pegs should fit tightly and once tapped into position they must be flush with the chair frame. If you plan to cover the frame holes with a cane beading [molding], do not do this pegging until the beading [molding] is in position.

Step Seven—beading [molding]: this is a fairly modern refinement and is an optional extra. It is a length of cane positioned around the outline of the weaving to give a neat finish. It can be put on with two different size canes, usually numbers two and six, though there is no set rule and number four can be used. The thicker cane is laid over the tops of the holes to hide them. Then the thicker cane is couched down with the thinner cane. Beading [molding] is combined with either pegging or tying in. Tie in before starting the beading [molding].

Start the beading [molding] by inserting a length of number two cane in a hole next to a corner. Allow the end to protrude 38 mm ($1\frac{1}{2}$ in) towards the top. Bend this end down into the next hole and bring the long end up through the same hole. This method will secure the short end. Insert a length of number six cane down into the same hole and position it so that it lies over the holes along that side of the chair frame. Pass the thinner cane over the thick cane and take it down the same hole. Pass this thin cane to the next hole on the underside—always the untwisted, glossy side facing you—and up through that hole. Take it over the thick cane and then down the same hole. Continue to the corner hole and insert the thick and the thin cane into this hole. Start the two canes for beading [molding] along the adjacent side before pegging the ends finally. Repeat all around to complete. Finally trim all ends underneath after making sure they are all tied or pegged. If the holes are very close together you will find it easier to do the beading

[molding] with number four cane, otherwise couch the thick cane down through alternate holes instead of every hole.

Finishing

There is no need to leave cane in its natural colour, even though this is attractive and blends with most colour [decorating] schemes. It can be painted with acrylic paint; this is flexible even when dry and will not flake off. You will find that plain colours like black, white and red look far better than pastels.

Cane is not just for chair seats. A well-caned panel has an extremely smart appearance that makes it useful for many other decorative situations.

Occasional tables can be given cane tops, which should be made of thick number six cane for strength, and are probably best protected with glass as well. If the table frame with its top removed and suitable holes drilled all around will not do, you can easily make a wooden frame the same size as the original top and paint or polish it to match the table before applying the cane. Cane screens have a very attractive light appearance, and do, in fact, let quite a lot of light through, which makes them useful as room dividers in dimly-lit rooms. The best way of making the large area involved is to make a number of frames, cane them, and set them into a wooden framework.

The same type of frame can be used for wall panels. Square frames are the easiest to make and the quickest to cane—a worthwhile point when you have a lot of caning to do. Door panels look interesting with caned insets made to cover the panels. This is a good way of giving a lighter look to a heavy-looking door. An ugly radiator can be masked by a box frame filled with caned panels that will let the heat through, but it is advisable to put a thick blockboard shelf on top. Cane headboards for beds look light and attractive. You can add a caned panel to a boring solid headboard. Make a frame like a straight-edged picture frame, drill holes, cane it and fix in place.

Rush

Most households have a few old chairs with sound wooden frames but worn-out bottoms. Apart from re-upholstering or re-caning, you might consider bringing the old friend back into service with a new rush seat. Rushing is easy, quick and relatively inexpensive; it is a good way of giving a new seat to a square or rectangular frame and you will get an attractive rustic look that blends well with the simple lines of modern furniture.

Get into practice by plaiting [braiding] and weaving rushes before tackling your seating problem. Make an attractive set of table mats to try your hand and get some experience of handling rush.

Rush mats have a long history. In Tudor times in England rushes were strewn on the floor so that people could walk more comfortably on the cold stones, but in this loose form they soon became broken and messy. So, in time, the women of the house learned to plait or braid the rushes into mats which lasted longer and looked tidier. Much later rush mats found their way on to the dinner table. Rush floor mats are still used and are suitable for many homes, especially country cottages. Weaving rush mats is not difficult, once you learn to handle the rushes and many lovely patterns can be made and invented. Choose thick rushes for floor matting and fine rushes for table mats. Rushes used to be widely grown for the purpose, but are now often imported from the Middle East. Rushes grow in still waters and slow moving rivers. Once harvested, they are left to dry slowly. They are then tied into 'bolts' and sold as such. The lengths of the rushes in a bolt vary—the average length is about 183 cm (6 ft). Rushes should be stored in a dry, airy place, preferably in the dark, so that the colour does not fade. Be careful how you handle the rushes when they are dry as they are very brittle and damage easily. Before using

Opposite: learn how to handle natural rushes and make these handsome chunky rush mats for your dining table.

them, wet them for about five minutes, either by sprinkling with a hose or a watering can in the garden, or by dipping them in a bath of cold water. Wrap them in a wet blanket or burlap sacking for a further three hours, or overnight.

Preparation

Each rush must be prepared before use. The thin end must be tested for strength. Hold a rush in both hands about 15 cm (6 in) down from the brown flowery top (or thin end, if it has lost its flower) and pull it apart with a gentle tug. Discard the broken end and try again another 15 cm (6 in) down, until the rush is quite firm and does not snap. It is much less frustrating to get rid of the weak bits first than to have the rushes snap as you work with them. Each rush must now be 'wiped'. This is partly to clean the rush and partly to remove all the air and water from inside the stem. Hold the stem in one hand at the thin end and, with a damp cloth in the other hand, wipe this along the rush, pressing it flat at the same time, so that the water runs out of the thick end. If this is not done, the work will shrink too much after weaving.
Rush plaiting or braiding: select three rushes and tie them together somewhere in the middle, but not in half, or the ends will all run out at the same time and make the joining of new rushes difficult. Fine, strong string or linen thread is used to tie the rushes. Always leave the ends of the string long enough to allow for sewing later on.

Loop the rushes at the point where they are tied together, around a hook or nail in the wall. Bring the six ends together and divide them into three pairs, so that each pair has a thick and a thin end. This will keep the thickness of the plait or braid even. Although the plaiting looks just the same as braided hair, in rush work only the right hand is used for the actual work. The left hand merely holds the material.

Hold two of the pairs in the left hand. Using the right hand, twist the other pair two or three times to the right, stroking and pulling the

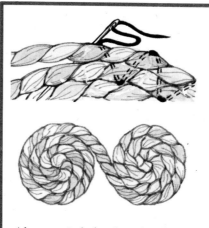

Above: *stitch the plaited rushes as you coil them into the shapes you need for round or oval mats. Add decorative coils in the centres.*

rushes at the same time, so that the two rushes look like one and are quite firm. Place the right hand pair over the top of the centre pair and hold under the left thumb. Pass the left hand pair over the top of the twisted rushes. The original right hand pair is now the left hand pair, the left hand pair is in the centre and the centre pair is now the right hand pair. This pair is now ready to be worked by the right hand. Continue twisting the right hand rushes as before, with the right hand, then placing the rushes in the left hand by taking them over the centre pair. The left hand pair is then placed over it so that the centre pair is on the right. Keep the width of the plait or braid even. A marker can be used by slipping a ring of the required size over the work. If it gets thicker, the ring will not slip down along the plait or braid, and if it gets thinner, the ring will become too loose.

To join in a new rush, wait until the end to be replaced is about 10 cm (4 in) long and in the centre of the work. Lay the new rush against the old so that the top end of the new rush protrudes 75 mm (3 in). When it is their turn, twist all three together, working with the old and the new. Continue working until the short end of the old rush is lost in the plait. Generally, a thick end should be replaced by a thick end, and a thin with a thin in order to keep the work even. At all times

aim to keep the combined thickness of the six rushes even. After working a length, cut off all the ends of the new rushes as closely as possible to the plait [braid], together with any old ends which may show. Short lengths are suitable for table mats, but floor mats will require a much longer plait or braid.

Table mats

For a small round table mat, about 20 cm (8 in) in diameter, plait or braid for about 4.6 m (5 yd). Make the work 13 mm ($\frac{1}{2}$ in) thick. Do not finish off the ends. Press it flat by passing it through a wringer or by placing it between a newspaper and putting some heavy books on top.

You will need:
- Blanket to wrap rushes, cloth to wipe them
- Scissors
- String or thread, fine and coarse, if necessary
- Large eye needle
- Rush threader or football lacing awl to thread ends into the work

Stitching: thread the string at the beginning of the plait on to a needle. Make a tight coil, with the flat part of the plait [braid] forming the thickness of the mat. Stitch in position through the mat. Do not worry if the plait or braid is not long enough for your requirements: re-wet the ends and continue with the rope for as long as you wish. Many rushworkers make the mats by plaiting [braiding] a length and then stitching the work before continuing.

To join in a new thread, tie the old and the new threads together with a reef knot and continue to sew, pulling the knot through the rushes until the old thread is used up. To finish off a mat cut off the underneath rush from each pair and weave the remaining three rushes into the plait [braid] of the previous row. Push the rush threader through the last three rows of plait

Opposite: *a modern classic, the scarlet Magistretti chair, gets a traditionally classic seat with natural rushes.*

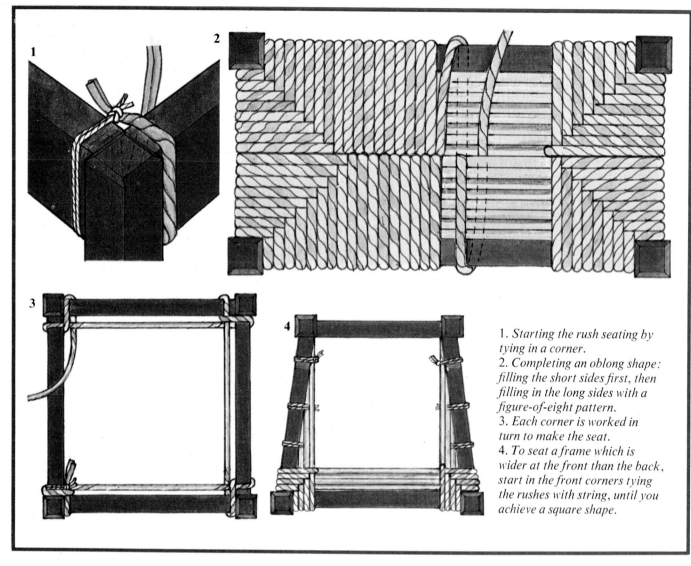

1. *Starting the rush seating by tying in a corner.*
2. *Completing an oblong shape: filling the short sides first, then filling in the long sides with a figure-of-eight pattern.*
3. *Each corner is worked in turn to make the seat.*
4. *To seat a frame which is wider at the front than the back, start in the front corners tying the rushes with string, until you achieve a square shape.*

or braid, thread the rush into the eye of the threader and pull it into the work.

Oval mats: to make an oval mat about 25 × 35 cm (10 × 14 in) plait [braid] for 11 m (12 yd). Begin the centre coil by doubling back the end and stitching into position. The piece doubled back should equal the difference between the width and length required—in this case, 10 cm (4 in). Continue to stitch the plait [braid] around this elongated coil which will form an oval. Finish as before.

Coils: the mats can be made more interesting by adding a series of coils.

For coils make a length of plait [braid] and mark the centre. Coil and stitch from one end towards the centre. Stitch in the usual way. Bind the other end with thread and then stitch towards the centre so that the two coils are opposite to

each other. It is usual to have an odd number of coils, so that the end of the last one is continued to form the plaiting [braiding] around the outside. In this way the ugly look of a join is avoided.

Re-seating a chair

Old chairs are often sold inexpensively because the rush seats need replacing. An average chair takes about three-quarters of a rush bolt to re-seat. No further special equipment is necessary.

Preparation: strip off all the old rushes and do any repairs to the framework of the chair. Re-finish the chair if need be; it will be almost impossible to do this when the new seating is in place. Prepare the rushes as before.

A square chair or stool is started by tying two rushes—one thick end and one thin end—to a corner on the left side rail with string. Make

sure this is very secure. Take the two rushes in the right hand and twist them to the right, stroking and pulling them quite firmly at the same time so that the two rushes look like one. Take the twisted rushes over and down the front rail at the corner. Now pass the rushes under the front rail and up through the chair untwisted. Twist the rushes to the left this time, stroke, pull and twist, and then take them over the first twist, over and down the left side rail. Pass under the left side rail and across to the right side rail, untwisted. Turn the chair around so that you can now repeat the looping process in this corner. Work each corner in this way. The first twist in each corner is always to the right, and the second one to the left. You may prefer to think of it as always twisting away from the corners. Try to use your right hand to do the right twist and your left hand to do the left twist. Keep the diagonal lines of the pattern at an angle of 45° from each corner and make sure that each twisted pair is parallel to the side rails. Join in a new rush by tying the old end and the new together with a reef knot.

Try to keep all knots on the untwisted section between the rails where they will be covered and so hidden. At first this will be easy but it becomes more difficult as the work goes on. At the end, the knots will show underneath the chair, so keep them as neat as possible and turn the ends into the work.

Continue around the chair for about twelve rounds. Then it is time to start 'packing'. This is to make the rush work quite firm and even, and prevents the chair rails cutting the rushes. Turn the chair upside down. Use any left-overs of dry rush; ends that have been trimmed, weak pieces, spotted rushes and so on are all used up at this point. Cut them into short lengths and stuff them into the eight pockets, two at each corner, formed by the pattern of the work so far. Push them right into the corners and make the padding quite firm and tight. Use a knife handle to help push the packing into the work. Continue to rush the seat, but do not attempt to do the whole seat in one session. The rushes should be allowed to dry, and can then be pushed up closer together when starting work again. This helps to tighten up the seat. Pad every dozen or so rounds and try to keep the rushes very tight. When the centre is reached, tie the last one to the one opposite, underneath the chair.

Oblong shapes are started in the same way as a square seat. Work until the short side is filled up. Then continue to fill the long sides with a figure-of-eight pattern between the two long sides.

For a chair with the front rail longer than the back rail (that is, whose front is wider than its back), start as before, around the front two corners only, then tie the ends firmly against the right hand rail. Now start all over again at the left side and weave only around the front two corners and tie off. Con-

tinue in this way until the area still to be rushed is exactly square. Pad the corners if necessary. Then continue as before, working over the tie-in pieces.

Seagrass seating
It is not always possible to obtain rushes suitable for seat repairing. A thoroughly good alternative is seagrass. This is a tough, fibrous material, shiny and pale green or beige in colour. You buy it already twisted into a continuous cord, like string, unlike rushes which arrive in a bundle and have to be twisted together. Seagrass is stronger, more flexible and cleaner to use than

Above: *modern seagrass seating in a traditional pattern can work well.*

rushes, so you may prefer to use it anyway.

You will need:
• No special tools or equipment

It will speed your work with seagrass if you make some wooden 'shuttles' to wind the lengths of grass on. Make them from very thin wood—use orange crates or 3mm ($\frac{1}{8}$in) plywood, cut into a rectangle about 23×5 cm (9×2 in) cutting a deep V-shaped notch at each end— so that the grass can be wound on lengthwise.

You will need two hanks of seagrass to re-seat a large chair.

Preparation

Strip the chair, renovate and repolish. Wind the seagrass on the shuttles and soak in cold water for half-an-hour to make the seagrass easier to work with.

The seat is made the same way as with rushes, except that you are passing a shuttle full of seagrass through the frame instead of pieces of rush. Pull the seagrass as tight as you can and pack the rows of loops tightly on the frame sides by forcing them together with a screwdriver. You may find it easier on the hands to wear working gloves.

If your seat is wider at the front than the back, you can overcome this problem by broadening the row of loops along the front rail. Every *alternate* time the knotting process comes around to the front, instead of looping the grass under the frame and immediately passing it to the side, loop it around *twice,* and then pass it to the side. When knotting the second front corner, make the same type of double loop around the front frame rail. The first time around the frame, the two front corner knots should be normal (that is, single), the second time they should be doubled, the third time normal, and so on. As soon as this alternate double looping process has compensated for the slant of the sides and the gap in the middle of the seat is square or rectangular, stop doing it and carry on normally. The double looped section will hardly show if you press the rows together tightly enough at both front and back, though there will inevitably be a slight curve in the shaped row of knots.

Alternate patterns

A different pattern can be used and varied if desired on seats with a square frame, or the ready made unfinished stools specially made for this craft.

You will need:

• A length of dowel 13 mm ($\frac{1}{2}$ in) in diameter and slightly longer than the length of the chair frame

Seagrass seating

1. *Seagrass is best wound on small wooden 'shuttles' which you can make yourself, to make it easier to thread through the frame of the chair.*

2. *When making the first knot, hold the end of the seagrass in your left hand to stop it from slipping.*

3. *When you have looped the strand first round the front, then the left frame members, move on to the next corner.*

4. *The knot in the next corner should be made in exactly the same way as the first knot, but there is no need to hold the end.*

5. *Here the first few rows are completed. The strands have not yet tightened together by sliding them along the frame, so you have a slightly irregular look.*

6. *When you come to the end of one piece of seagrass, tie on the next piece so that the knot comes under the seat.*

7. *Any projecting strands that refuse to lie flat can be pulled down by looping a strand round them from underneath.*

8. *When seating a chair that is wider at the front than the back, loop alternate knots round the front frame twice. This can also be done round the sides to deepen the seat if need be.*

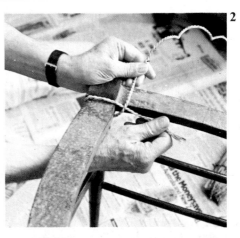

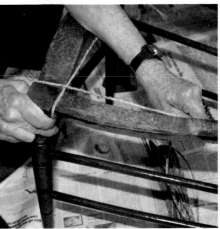

You will find it easier to work the second stage with the seagrass threaded through a large needle (or one made out of a wire coat hanger with two ends twisted together.

First stage: mark the centre of each side of the frame and make sure that you weave the same number of rounds on either side of the marks. Tie the end of the seagrass, on the underside, to the frame. Place the dowel across the centre of the frame at right angles to the direction in which you are working. Loop the seagrass (on the shuttle) up and around the front rail twice. Take it across to the opposite side on the underside of the frame and wind it around the frame twice. Return to the front on top of the frame. Take the next four rounds straight around the frame, without the double rounds, going from front to back on the underside and back to front on the top. Repeat the two wraps (or double loops) on each side, then repeat the four straight rounds. Proceed in this way across the frame, remembering to check that you have the same number of strands on either side of the halfway marks. End the weaving with double loops at front and back. If there is a long length of seagrass left, take it around to the adjacent side, on the inside of the frame, to begin the second stage, otherwise tie it in on the underside of the frame and start a new length of seagrass for the second stage. Remove the length of dowel.

Second stage: this is worked similarly to the first stage, but the seagrass should be threaded on a needle. The shuttle can be used initially, but as the weaving progresses, a needle will be more suitable. Make two double rounds to start with, then weave under the first four strands and over the next four and repeat the double loops at the opposite rail. Return on the underside, weaving under and over as before. Weave four straight rounds and then repeat the double loops. When weaving the top, you will find it easier if you use the

dowel to raise the alternate four strands going in the opposite direction so that you can pass the needle through easily to the other end.

Joining in, should it be necessary, must be done on the underside. Tie the old end and the new ends together so that the knot will be hidden on the underside of the frame.

The pattern is simple to alter: instead of two double loops and four straight rounds, you can do a variety of combinations, such as one and three, or two and five, and so on.

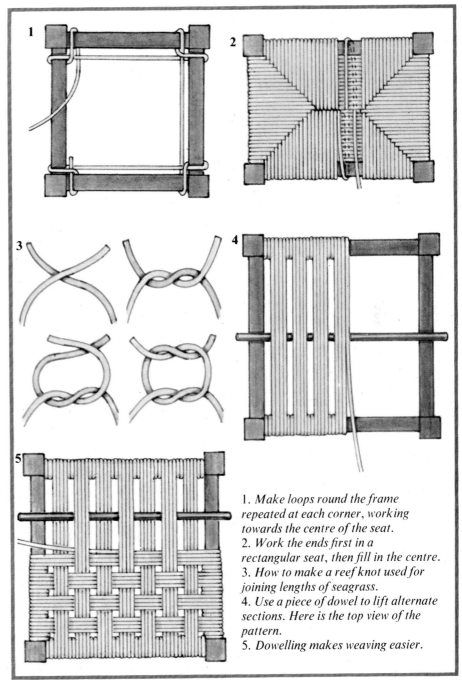

1. *Make loops round the frame repeated at each corner, working towards the centre of the seat.*
2. *Work the ends first in a rectangular seat, then fill in the centre.*
3. *How to make a reef knot used for joining lengths of seagrass.*
4. *Use a piece of dowel to lift alternate sections. Here is the top view of the pattern.*
5. *Dowelling makes weaving easier.*

Opposite: *seagrass stools in varied patterns make child-proof furnishings.*

Upholstery

Introduction to Upholstery

Mastering the traditional art of upholstery, or tackling the re-upholstery of a bedraggled piece of furniture needs patience, practice and can take a long time. However, all kinds of traditional chairs and sofas, no matter how grubby, sagging or tattered they may look, can be rescued, stripped and re-made to live long, useful and decorative lives. The materials are still comparatively cheap; modern substitutions making the task easier in some cases and the basic tools quite simple to use. Evening classes will take you painstakingly through each step until you acquire the know-how you need. Begin with something basic, such as a simple dining chair: do not tackle that deep-buttoned chesterfield until you know what you are doing.

A framed wooden skeleton still forms the base of most upholstered furniture—beech is most frequently used because it is strong and does not split easily under stress. Steel or some alternative form of springing is attached to the frame and covered with hessian [burlap] and one of a wide variety of stuffings. Horsehair and flocking have tended lately to be replaced by synthetics such as latex or plastic foam, because the natural materials are increasingly scarce and inconsistent in quality. Rubber webbing has replaced traditional flax. The skills of upholstery came into their own in Victorian times with elaborate, over-stuffed furniture and intricate buttoning. This type of furniture, still to be found in both junk and antique shops, usually had individual metal coil springs lashed to a canvas webbing base, covered with layers of hair and wadding [padding], plus elaborate braids.

Upholstery fabrics

Fabrics used in upholstered furniture and in loose or fitted covers may be divided into two categories: natural and synthetic.

Natural fibres

Cotton and cotton-based materials such as brocade, canvas, chintz, corduroy, sailcloth and duck are hard-wearing and practical. They are fairly easy to clean and are usually used for modern furniture or as loose covers for old furniture.

Less tough cotton-based fabrics include chenille, cotton velvet and velour. They are comfortable, look luxurious, but are not quite as practical as the tightly-woven, tougher cottons. Linen is another natural fibre used for loose cover fabrics, and so is linen union, a mixture of linen and cotton [linen rayon].

Wool-based fabrics in weaves such as bouclé, hopsacking and tweed are soft and comfortable to sit on, and can be chosen in colours and patterns that age attractively and do not show the dirt. Looser weaves, however, do not wear as well as close ones. Today's fabrics often combine the comfort and dirt-shedding quality of natural fibres with the hard-wearing ones of the synthetics.

Synthetic fibres

Those used for upholstery include nylon, the acrylics, the polyesters and the vinyls, under various trade names. They can give the look of luxurious, expensive natural materials with easy-care and hard-wearing qualities.

Luxury upholstery materials

These include silk brocade, damask, faille and moire, (often used on antique upholstered pieces), fur, satin, suede and leather. In practical terms, these can be beyond most people's means, but if you learn to upholster you might work on a special piece of furniture to add a touch of extravagance to your room.

Care of upholstered furniture

Upholstery is often the most neglected area in the house when it comes to regular cleaning—probably because dust and dirt show less. Both are great enemies of fabrics, lodging on furniture just as on the mantelpiece or sideboard.

Vacuum your upholstery regularly. It is a good idea to give your pieces a gentle beating with a short cane to bring dust and grit to the surface before you vacuum. Use an upholstery brush or special attachment to get into the crevices around the sides and backs. Ground-in dirt here can wear the fabric. Use a specific upholstery shampoo for all-over cleaning; others will leave a sticky residue which cannot easily be removed and encourages re-soiling. A dry foam cleaner is best as you need to clean the surfaces without soaking the upholstery. Follow the instructions carefully and allow ample time to dry. Do not try to hurry up the drying process by applying direct heat to the furniture; this can cause serious damage. Imitation leather made of vinyl can be wiped over with soapy water and dried off immediately with a soft cloth. Do not use polish: it makes a sticky surface build-up on the vinyl. Luxury fabrics in natural fibres are best tackled professionally.

Drop-in Dining Chair Seat

The drop-in seat of an ordinary dining chair is the easiest form of re-upholstery and a good introduction to the basic techniques of the craft. If you are successful, the same principles can be applied to larger pieces of furniture. If you plan to renovate a set of chairs, it is worth buying or borrowing the correct tools. Substitutes can be used, but the work will not be so easy.

You will need:
- Tape measure
- Shears, which should be really sharp, for cutting out fabric and other materials
- Mallet and ripping chisel [tack remover] for lifting the heads of tacks when removing old upholstery. The tip is blunted to prevent damage to the wood frame, and should always be driven in the direction of the grain and inwards from corners to avoid splitting or marring the wood. Use it to remove staples
- Tack lifter or nail puller for pulling out the tacks. You could use carpenter's pincers, or long-nosed pliers, a tack hammer or the claw end of a nail hammer
- G [C] clamps are useful for holding the chair base firmly to your work surface
- Upholsterer's hammer with a face about 15 mm ($\frac{5}{8}$ in) and claw at the other end. A reasonable

substitute would be a carpenter's 'pin' hammer. A cabriole or framing hammer is another specialized tool used for delicate tacking work along polished edges and carving
- Web strainer or stretcher used for stretching the webbing across the seat of the chair to prevent sagging. You can improvise one from a clothes peg or a narrow piece of hardwood around which the webbing can be wrapped and pulled taut if you have a strong wrist

- Upholsterers' tacks with flat heads are used to attach the various materials to the frame. Nails should never be used; their heads are too small. Use 13 mm ($\frac{1}{2}$ in) [4 or 6 oz] fine or 13 mm ($\frac{1}{2}$ in) [8 or 12 oz] 'improved' for a drop-in seat. For the webbing on easy chairs, 15 mm ($\frac{5}{8}$ in) [20 oz] tacks are used
- Plastic wood or wood putty for filling old tack holes if these will show
- Cloth-backed strong tape 38 mm ($1\frac{1}{2}$ in) wide as long as the total

Here are some of the special tools which make upholstering easier.
Top: *web strainer or stretcher and webbing, tape measure, two sizes of tacks.*
Bottom, left to right: *shears, mallet, ripping chisel [tack remover], tack lifter [nail puller], cabriole [framing] hammer.*

Above: *this dining chair is ideal for the beginner in upholstering.*

outside measurement of the chair seat plus 10 cm (4 in)
- Latex-based adhesive
- Webbing: the highest grade of webbing is made from pure flax and is black and white with a twill weave. Other grades are made from jute and cotton or hemp, are brown in colour, and sometimes linen threads are woven into the selvedges [selvages] for strength. Plain or striped brown webbing is a cheaper grade made from jute and not recommended for dining chairs. Rubberized webbing is useful for some types of re-upholstery but is an extravagance for a simple dining chair seat (see page 91 for details of rubber webbing).

Webbing is placed across the seat frame in strands, running in both directions, and is interwoven to support the seat padding. Most chairs have two strands each way but each chair should be examined to make sure that you buy enough to duplicate the original arrangement. Allow 50 mm (2 in) extra for overlap on each strand.
- Padding: foam padding is very suitable and should be 50 mm (2 in) deep and 13 mm ($\frac{1}{2}$ in) larger

all round than the chair seat. Use latex (rubber) or polyether [polyurethane] foam.

Traditionally dining chairs were stuffed with horsehair padded with wool, but today, these materials are difficult to find and use. Foam padding is a practical and good alternative. Choose latex (rubber) if possible—it comes in cavity, plain or pin-core slabs or sheets—but, it is worth noting that polyether [polyurethane] is less expensive and easier to find. Both are available in various densities and thicknesses. For areas subject to much wear, you will need high density foam—27-30.5 kg per cu m (1.5-1.8 lbs per cu ft) [2.15-2.55 lbs per cu ft]—while for places which do not take much pressure (such as the inside of armchair arms, bedroom chair seats and so on) you can use a lower density—21-28 kg per cu m (1.1-1.5 lbs per cu ft) [1.25-1.45 lbs per cu ft]. Thickness also depends on the amount of use the area will have and the overall effect required. Foam for seating should be thick enough not to compress uncomfortably when in use.

Foam for building up the shape of seats, arms and chair backs can be thinner. You will need to attach strips of tape or calico [muslin] around the edges of the foam to provide anchorage. Upholstery wadding [padding]—which can be a sort of flock cotton wool or cotton batting, or a washable synthetic wadding [padding]—can also be added for an extra-soft, luxurious look and feel.

Safety note
All upholstery materials, modern or traditional, will burn and give off noxious gases if there is a fire in your home. Foams catch fire more quickly than horsehair and other traditional stuffings and it is not easy for the do-it-yourselfer to buy flame-retardant varieties. Wool upholstery fabrics help retard fire, and clean fabrics are less likely to catch fire: greasy surfaces are very inflammable. Try not to make any crevices in your upholstery which could easily hide a smouldering cigarette end.

Calculating the cover fabric
Choose a fabric which is hard-wearing, closely-woven and non-fraying, so that it will be easy to work with and to clean. If you choose a fabric with a large pattern or motif, you will have to buy enough to allow for the central placing of the pattern on a set of matching chairs. Plain fabric is more economical.

To calculate the amount of fabric needed for each chair, measure the length and width of the seat at the widest part and allow at least 15 cm (6 in) on each measurement so that the fabric can be folded over the seat frame. You will also need a piece of hessian [burlap] and two pieces of calico [muslin] or linen 50 mm (2 in) wider and longer than the seat for each chair.

Stripping the seat
Cover your work surface with newspaper, remove the seat from the chair and secure it, upside down, to the work surface with G [C] clamps.

Using the ripping chisel [tack remover] and mallet (or your substitute tools), start to drive out the tacks holding the bottom hessian [burlap] and cover fabric. To do this, place the tip of the chisel behind the head of the tack and tap it out, working with the grain of the wood to avoid splitting. Use the claw side of the hammer, or a pair of pliers or pincers to pull it out completely.

Next, turn the seat over and remove the cover and stuffing. Cut any twine ties with scissors. Strip off the hessian [burlap] and webbing in the same way. If a piece of plywood has been used as a base, remove all the nails holding this. As you work, note the way the webbing was originally placed, the side of the frame to which it was tacked, and the part of the frame which was uppermost when finished. Examine the frame carefully and remove all old tacks. Treat woodworm holes if necessary. If the new fabric is thicker than the original, plane down the frame a little to allow for the added thickness.

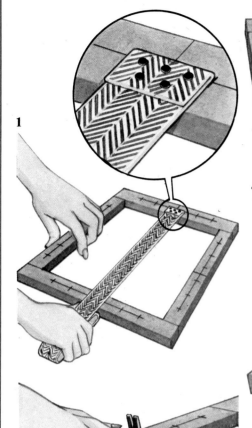

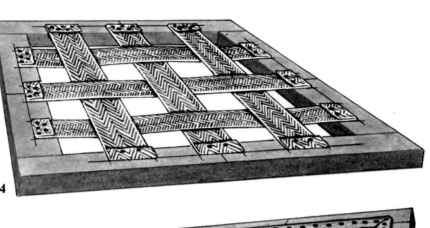

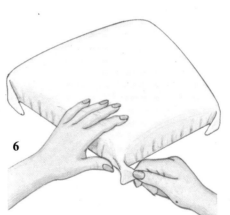

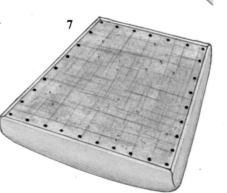

Drop-in dining chair seat

1. *Tack down the first webbing strand (close-up shows the position of the tacks).*

2. *Strain and tack down the end of the strand to the front rail.*

3. *Fold over the end of the webbing and secure with more tacks.*

4. *Add the rest of the webbing strands, interlacing them as shown, and tacking them down in the same way.*

5. *Tack down a piece of hessian [burlap] over the webbing.*

6. *After forming the seat shape, pull fabric over the frame edge and tack in place, being careful to pleat the corners evenly. Temporary or stay-tack in place, and adjust if necessary before driving tacks home.*

7. *Attach the back hessian [burlap] folding in the raw edges for a neat look.*

Left: *a renovated dining chair seat.*

completely dry, place the foam on the hessian [burlap], tape side up and, holding it firmly in position, tack the free edge of the tape to the frame. As the foam is slightly larger than the seat, it will make a dome in the centre, giving a rounded shape to the finished seat. For an even higher dome, place an additional piece of foam in the centre, tapering the edges with a bread-knife.

The foam should now be covered with a piece of calico [muslin] or linen to give a firm foundation to the cover fabric. Attach this in the same way as the hessian [burlap] covering the webbing, but cut off the raw edges close to the tacks, and place the new row of tacks below those holding the tape in place.

Adding the cover fabric

Place the cover fabric on the work surface, wrong side facing you. Place the seat, foam side down on the fabric, making sure it is centred, and pull up the fabric edges over the sides, to the bottom of the seat frame, holding the centre of each side with a temporary or stay-tack. Working from the centre of the back to each side, fix with a row of tacks, then, pulling the fabric taut, fix the front edge with a row of tacks in the same way. Fix the sides, working out to the corners. From time to time, turn the seat over carefully to check that the fabric grain is straight. It must run true from front to back, and the sides at exact right angles.

At the corners, make a double pleat. First pull the point firmly down and tack it. Fold the excess fabric into inverted pleats and tack these down. Cut off any excess fabric bulk. Cover the bottom of the chair seat with the remaining piece of calico [muslin] or linen, folding under the raw edges, spacing the tacks that hold it to the frame to cover the raw edges and the tacks which hold the seat cover to the frame.

Replace the newly-covered seat in the chair frame.

Replacing the webbing

Space the webbing evenly. If there is an uneven number of webbing strips, start with the centre front to back piece.

Without cutting off a length of webbing, place the end of the webbing on the top of the frame on the back side, cut side of the webbing facing inwards. Tack it down with five tacks, placed in a 'W' shape. Stretch the webbing across to the front of the frame, pressing the edge of the strainer [stretcher] on the side of the frame to give leverage. Tack the webbing, again using three tacks in a straight line. Cut off the webbing with 25 mm (1 in) to spare, turn it back over the first tacks and tack again with two tacks in the same 'W' shape (the first three tacks will be hidden by the fold).

Fix the other pieces of webbing from the back to the front of the frame in the same way, then secure the pieces of webbing which run across the seat, interlacing the strips with the other webbing.

Mark the centre of each edge of one hessian [burlap] piece. Place in position on the frame over the webbing, aligning the centres. Attach temporarily at the centres with a tack hammered halfway down. Then, making sure that the fabric grain is kept straight, working from the centre of each side towards the corners, place tacks about 38 mm (1½ in) apart, pulling hessian [burlap] taut. Turn up the raw edges and tack these down.

Attaching the padding

Cut four pieces of tape, equal in length to the sides of the foam, plus 25 mm (1 in). Fold the tape in half lengthways and crease firmly. Glue one side of the folded tape to the outside edge of the foam, position-ing the crease as shown. When

Renovating a Fireside Chair

Fireside chairs—small easy chairs with a padded back and seat and open wooden arms—can often be bought inexpensively in junk shops. They are easy to renovate with sprung or foam upholstery, give you good practice in handling basic upholstery techniques and materials, and the opportunity to acquire the tools and the confidence you need to tackle more elaborate jobs.

Styles of fireside chair

While not as comfortable as fully upholstered chairs, these small chairs have long been popular as extra chairs in a sitting room or bedroom, or for small rooms when a conventional chair would look too bulky. With some, the upholstery consists simply of two removable cushions, one for the seat and one for the back. This style is the simplest of all to renovate, because you simply replace any worn or missing springs, padding if necessary, and re-cover the cushions.

On some styles of chair, the padding is fixed permanently on the back and there is a separate removable cushion for the seat. With other styles, both the back and seat may be fully upholstered. But with all these styles, the basic methods can be adapted to suit your own chair.

Types of cover

There are two main styles for covering the back of a fireside chair. Most commonly, the cover fabric on the inside back wraps around the side edges to the outside back of the frame and is tacked there. A separate piece of fabric is cut to cover the outside back. This gives the sides of the chair a rounded look. Alternatively, a piece of fabric is cut to fit the inside back only and separate pieces—like the welt strips of a box cushion—are joined on to cover the depth of the padding at the sides. This gives a squarer, more tailored look to the chair.

Right: a beginner can confidently tackle a plain-lined fireside chair.

89

Stripping the chair

It is usually easiest to strip off the old upholstery before you buy any new materials so that you can see how the upholstery was constructed, which pieces can be re-used and which will need replacing.

When stripping the back of a chair with fixed upholstery, remove the back panel first. If stitched, remove the stitches carefully. You will then be able to see the tacks for the front panel. Remove these. Staples can be prised [pried] up with the sharp point of a basic tool. Next examine the padding. Keep any genuine horsehair for future, if not immediate, re-use. Strip off and throw away any padding which is compressed and thin or crumbling. If the padding is in good condition leave it in place, unless the springing, webbing or hessian [burlap] underneath it needs replacing. You can check this without removing the padding, by looking through the outside back of the frame.

The seat

Remove the cover fabric from the seat cushion and examine the cushion pad. Re-use it if in good condition and comfortable.

The springing

Check the springing under the seat cushion. Most fireside chairs have either tension springs (tightly-coiled, narrow springs which cross the frame from side to side and slip into metal clips on each side) or rubber webbing. There may also be springs or webbing on the back of the chair. Frayed or torn rubber webbing can be replaced. If the tension springs are sound, but the metal strip holes are worn, these can be re-drilled and re-fixed. On the other hand, you can remove metal springing and replace with rubber webbing. These materials can be obtained from an upholsterer's supplier.

Opposite: *before and after. The small top picture shows a solid, dreary chair. The big picture shows what a new cover and a coat of fresh paint can do to transform it.*

Preparing the frame

Treat the frame for woodworm if necessary, allowing two or three days for it to dry. Repair loose joints by scraping out as much of the old glue as possible, squeezing new woodworking adhesive into the crevice and clamping the joint firmly until dry. If the join will not show, you can give additional strength with a metal or wood plate. Spruce up the show-wood, strip and re-finish or paint, according to its condition.

You will need:

- For stripping: tack hammer and lifter, scissors or upholstery ripper, wood renovation materials (see p. 33-45) ripping chisel [tack remover] and mallet
- Basic equipment: general purpose latex adhesive for attaching foam to calico [muslin]; small curved upholstery needle and strong thread; scissors; regulator—this is a professional upholstery needle 20-25 cm (8-10 in long)—which helps to form the stuffing into a good shape, it has one pointed and one flat end. A kitchen skewer can be used but the regulator is inexpensive; staple gun (optional)
- Rubber webbing: to be used if you are replacing the springs. To calculate the amount of webbing you should buy for each length, measure the distance it will span and subtract 10 per cent for tensioning. If the lengths are attached with metal clips, add 25 mm (1 in) to each length to allow for fitting the clips.

The rubber webbing takes the place of the original webbing or springs. It is attached to the top of the seat frame. Mark the position for each strand on back, front and side rails, and smooth off the inner edges of the frame with sandpaper, so the webbing will not be abraded. Using the webbing straight from the roll, to avoid waste, place the first length in position, with the cut edge just inside the outside edge of the back chair rail. Tack it down, using five tacks placed in a line 6 mm

($\frac{1}{4}$ in) from the edge. Be careful to position the tacks at right angles to the frame, and to hammer them down so that the heads are completely flat against the webbing, so they cannot cut into it.

Each strand of webbing should be nine-tenths of the length of the distance it spans and then stretched to fit. So, after fixing the first strand at the back, mark the measurement on it and stretch it until the mark is in the middle of the front rail. Tack in position, placing the tacks on the mark. Cut off with 6 mm ($\frac{1}{4}$ in) to spare.

Attach the other front-to-back strands in the same way. The webbing is so strong that cross strands are not usually necessary, although one can be put at the back for extra support. Interlace it through the main webbing first, then tack one end. Mark the place where it reaches to the opposite rail unstretched, measure one-tenth of the total measurement back from this, stretch and tack down on the second mark.

- Metal clips: rubber webbing is sometimes fitted to wood frames with metal clips which grip the ends of the strands and are inserted into a slot in the chair frame. Buy two clips for each length of webbing you are replacing.
- Jute webbing, if needed: see p. 86 for calculation details
- Tacks: use 13 mm ($\frac{1}{2}$ in) improved tacks or brads for attaching webbing. Where the chair back is lined with hessian [burlap] rather than webbing, you will need enough 13 mm ($\frac{1}{2}$ in) improved tacks [brads] to place them 20 mm ($\frac{3}{4}$ in) around the edge of the frame
- Fine tacks: you will need about 450 gm (1 lb) of 10 mm ($\frac{3}{8}$ in) tacks for attaching all other layers
- Hessian [burlap]: for lining the inside back if necessary. Make a template (see below) for the amount you will need to buy and add 25 mm (1 in) all around for overlaps
- Foam: this is the easiest material to use for padding, whatever material may have been used

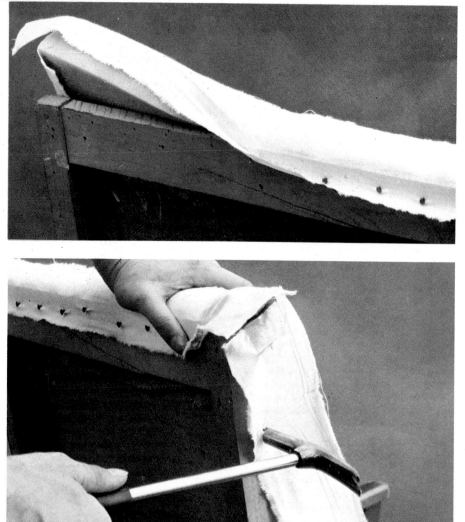

the seat cushion with two pieces from the seat template and a welt strip for each side. Allow extra length for positioning and matching any pattern and for cutting bias strips if you are adding piping or welting, then draw a line to complete the rectangle. Measure the length of the rectangle and convert back in scale to give the required amount of fabric. Another calculation method is on p. 86.

Piping: this is a strip of fabric cut on the bias, folded round a length of cord, used to make a plain seam look a little more interesting. The bias grain of a fabric runs diagonally across the fabric. This line can be found by folding the corner of the fabric over so that the cut edge runs parallel to the selvedge [selvage] edge. Crease along the diagonal fold and then cut along the crease line. Mark a line parallel with this cut edge further down the fabric. Mark the width of the piping (this should be three or four times as wide as the finished width you need) in chalk or pencil lines parallel to the cut edge. Fold the fabric into a tube (right sides together) so that the marked lines form a continuous spiral. Machine stitch the seam together and press open. Cut into a continuous bias strip along the marked lines. Fold over piping cord and machine stitch close to the cord.

Webbing and lining
Lining with hessian [burlap]

If you are lining the inside back with hessian [burlap], mark the centre point on each edge of the material and on each edge of the inside back of the frame. Place the cloth on the inside back, matching the centre points. Temporary or stay-tack it to the frame at each point. Keeping the grain of the hessian [burlap] straight, tack it along the centre of the top of the inside back frame, placing the tacks about 38 mm (1½ in) apart. Smooth it down to the bottom and tack down. Tack the sides in the same

originally. Use the template for calculating the quantity of 50 mm (2 in) foam you will need, adding 25 mm (1 in) all around. You may find your supplier will cut the foam to the template for you, otherwise use a breadknife or scissors. If the seat foam needs replacing, buy a piece no thinner than 75 mm (3 in) thick to the required size and shape

• Calico [muslin]: strips used for attaching the foam to the inside back of the chair and for covering the foam before the main cover fabric is attached. Buy enough material to cut a piece 15 cm (6 in) larger all around than the inside back template, plus enough for strips 10 cm (4 in) wide to fit around the outside edge of the inside back foam

Making a template
To calculate the size of the

materials to be used on the back of the chair, make a paper template of the exact shape. To do this, hold a piece of paper against the frame and mark the lines of the outside edge of the frame all around. Mark the position of the arms. If the seat cushion is not an exact rectangle, make a template of its shape.

Cover fabric
The safest way of estimating the amount needed is to make a cutting chart to scale. Draw an open ended rectangle with a width to represent the width of the cover fabric. Mark the piece for the inside back first, using the template as a guide, but making it 15 cm (6 in) larger all around than the template to allow for the depth of padding. Mark the piece for the outside back panel, using the inside back template as a guide, but making it 25 mm (1 in) larger all around to allow for turning under. Mark the pieces for

way. Turn back the raw edges of the cloth over the tacks and tack down, putting the tacks between those underneath.

Fitting rubber webbing
If rubber webbing must be attached with tacks, follow the method described on p. 91. If the frame has grooves for webbing clips, proceed as follows. Press one end of a webbing strand onto the teeth of the clip. If you have a carpentry vice [vise], place the clip in it and tighten carefully to close the clip over the webbing. Alternatively, use pliers to close the clip. Repeat at the opposite end of the strand. Place one clip in position in the groove and pull the webbing until you can insert the other clip in the opposite groove. Note: with some styles of chair it may be easier to replace the seat springing after the back upholstery is complete.

Jute webbing: If this was used, replace it, following the original arrangement and using the method detailed on p. 88.

Backs with rounded edges
Attaching the foam
Prepare the foam with calico [muslin] strips and attach it to the back of the frame, using the method of rolling the edges described on p. 88. Temporary or stay-tack the strips along the top of the outside back of the frame, placing the tacks 13 mm ($\frac{1}{2}$ in) from the outer edge of the frame and about 50 mm (2 in) apart.

Fitting round the arms
Cut horizontal slits in the material and foam to the inner edge of the arm and level with the centre of the arms. Squash the foam to fit above and below. Tack the calico [muslin] to the outside back down the sides.

Attaching the bottom edge
If the frame has a tack bar or rail—a separate piece of wood above the back rail of the seat—trim the calico [muslin] strip at each corner so that it can be pulled under the bar and tacked to the outside back. Where there is no bar, tack the calico [muslin] to the

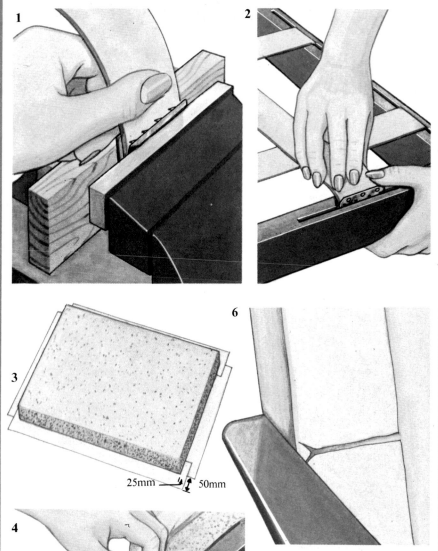

25mm — 50mm

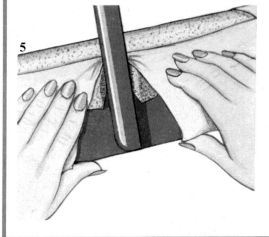

1. *If you need to replace the rubber webbing on your chair, you will need to fit a metal clip at each end of the piece. Use a vice [vise] to make this firm.*
2. *Slip the clips into the slots in the chair frame to hold the rubber webbing in place.*
3. *Attach calico [muslin] strips to the edges of the foam with adhesive.*
4. *Fix the foam to the chair with tacks. Pulling the calico [muslin] strips firmly before tacking, makes a rounded edge.*
5. *Cut and fit the calico [muslin] and foam around the arms of the chair.*
6. *Here is how to cut the material so that it will fit smoothly around the arms.*

inside face of the bottom rail. When you are satisfied with the placement of the foam, either drive home the tacks or use a staple gun.

Calico [muslin] cover

It is always better to cover the foam with calico [muslin] to give a smooth foundation for the main cover and to help protect the foam.

Using the inside back template as a pattern, cut out a piece of calico [muslin], allowing an extra 15 cm (6 in) all round. Place the material centrally over the foam, take the fabric edges around to the outside back of the frame and fix them with a temporary or stay-tack in the centre of each side. Add more of these tacks along the centre of the top rail at 50 mm (2 in) intervals to within 50 mm (2 in) of the corners, and smooth the calico [muslin] down to the bottom. If the frame has a tack bar, fit the material around the uprights and pull it through to the outside back. Temporary or stay-tack along the centre of the rail. If there is no bar, tack the material to the inside rail to within 50 mm (2 in) of the corners.

Fitting round the arms: to fit the calico [muslin] round the arms, remove the temporary or stay-tacks holding the side edges, and fold back the side edges level with the inner edges of the arms. Cut a horizontal slash into the material level with the centre of each arm from the raw edge to within 13 mm ($\frac{1}{2}$ in) of the fold. Then make two diagonal cuts up to the fold. Pull the calico [muslin] tightly round the sides of the frame, using the blunt end of the regulator or skewer to tuck the edges of the slash under the slit in the foam. Temporary or stay-tack the sides of the material to the outside back. When all the edges are temporary or stay-tacked and the lining is completely smooth and taut, either drive the tacks home or replace with staples. Finish each corner in a square pleat, cutting away the surplus fabric inside the pleat before tacking down.

The main cover

Cut out the fabric as for the calico [muslin] cover, being careful to place any design motif centrally. Attach the fabric as for the calico [muslin], but place the tacks 15 mm ($\frac{1}{2}$ in) in from the outer edge of the outside back frame. Slash the fabric at the arms as for the calico [muslin] and turn under the edges of the slash so that the folds are above and below the arms. Take the fabric around to the back of the frame and temporary or stay-tack. To make a neat finish, if there is an ugly gap behind the arms, cut two pieces of fabric 75 mm (3 in) square, matching the fabric design to the fabric above and below the gap if possible. Release two temporary or stay-tacks on each side of the arm and insert the cut square. Fold under its front edge and place in position behind the arms. Tack along the top and bottom edge. Re-tack the edges of the cover, folding under the bottom edge if there is no tack bar or rail. When you are satisfied with the placement of the cover, finish the corners with pleats and drive the tacks home or replace with staples.

Finishing the outside back: cut a piece of fabric for the outside back from the inside back template, allowing 13 mm ($\frac{1}{2}$ in) all around. Mark the centre point on each edge. Do the same on the frame, and then place the fabric in position, matching the centre points. Fold under the raw edges, so that the folds are just inside the edges of the frame and pin to the inside back fabric.

Slip or whip stitching

This is a technique commonly used in upholstery for attaching outside panels, such as the backs of chair covers.

Thread a curved needle with strong thread, and knot the free end. Insert the needle into the fold from the open end and pull out about 13 mm ($\frac{1}{2}$ in) further down. Make a straight stitch across to the fabric on the other side and make a small stitch towards the opening. Bring the needle out and make a straight stitch across to the fold. Run the needle along the fold in the direction of the area to be covered, making a stitch of about 13 mm

($\frac{1}{2}$ in). Make a small stitch across to the other side and make another 13 mm ($\frac{1}{2}$ in) stitch. Continue all round. If you prefer, the top edge of the outside back can be back-tacked (see p. 100) for a neat finish and the sides and bottom edges slip stitched.

Backs with squared edges

For this kind of chair, the side edges of foam are not squashed down to give a rounded look, so the foam should be cut only 13 mm ($\frac{1}{2}$ in) larger than the inside back template on these edges. 25 mm (1 in) should still be added to the top and bottom.

Fitting the foam: prepare the side edges of the foam with the calico [muslin] strips as for the drop-in dining chair seat, see p. 88. Prepare the top and bottom edges of the foam as for chairs with rounded edges. Attach the foam to the back of the chair, temporary or stay-tacking the calico [muslin] strips to the outside back.

Calico [muslin] cover

Using the inside back template as a pattern, cut out a piece of material to cover the foam, allowing 13 mm ($\frac{1}{2}$ in) extra on the side edges and 15 cm (6 in) at the top and bottom for turning under. For the welt strips cut a 15 cm (6 in) wide strip of calico [muslin] the length of the side edges of the main section. Mark the centres on one long edge of the welts and on the side edges of the main section. Pin the welts securely to the side edges of the main section, matching the centre points, to within 15 cm (6 in) of each end. Keeping the calico [muslin] with the wrong side out, try it in position on the chair. Temporary or stay-tack the top and bottom and the back edges of the welts. Cut into the welt strips as necessary to fit them around the arms and pin them to fit the shape of the main section at the top and bottom. Make any other adjustments. Take the lining off the chair. Mark the seam lines on both sides, unpin the seams and then use the pieces as a pattern for cutting out the main cover. Re-fit the calico [muslin] pieces together, machine stitch the seams and press the raw edges towards the welts. Trim to within 13 mm ($\frac{1}{2}$ in) of the stitching. Replace the calico [muslin], right side out, on the chair and tack.

Main cover

Make up the main cover as for the lining, but include piping in the seams joining the welts to the main section. Attach the outside back panel as for chairs with rounded edges.

The seat cushion

If the cushion is a rectangle, cut a piece of fabric (plus seam allowances) for each side, machine stitch edges together, fabric right side in, leaving one edge open, turn, insert the foam pad, slip stitch the open edge, turning the raw edges in. You might insert a zip [zipper] in one seam so that the cushion cover can be removed for cleaning. If the cushion is not a rectangle, cut the bottom and top pieces of the cover from your seat template, and welting strips to fit the edges of these pieces. Assemble as before.

Below: *a pot of paint, a few yards of a striking modern furniture fabric, makes this chair new again.*

Re-covering a
Modern Armchair

Here is how to re-cover modern armchairs and settees or sofas and how to replace the upholstery with foam—this works if the original upholstery was foam or traditional padding materials.

Foam upholstery

The major change in upholstery over the last decade is the increasing use of foam for the padding instead of 'loose' fillings such as horsehair and fibre or upholstery felt. Foam is both less expensive and easier to use than a loose filling, but it does not last as long and, in regular use, tends to lose its resilience and depth after a few years. Therefore, when the cover fabric needs replacing on chairs upholstered with foam, it often makes sense to replace the upholstery at the same time. If your furniture was upholstered by traditional methods, it probably does not need more than the wadding [padding] replaced, so you can simply follow the instructions for replacing the cover.

Of course, there are many different styles and shapes of easy chair, but the methods of construction are very similar and many of the basic principles are similar to those already described earlier in the book. However, as each chair may have different details, it is helpful to make notes as you strip off the old upholstery.

Stripping old upholstery

Do this before you buy any new materials, so that you can see exactly what you will need. Make notes and sketches as you work, on how each layer is attached to the frame.

The cover

Remove the piece of fabric on the underside of the chair, then the cover fabric, beginning with the outside back and arms, following the method described on p. 91. Make a careful note of any edges which were slip-stitched and back-tacked (for a description of these processes, see pp. 94 and 100).

Flies

When you remove the cover you may find that strips of hessian [burlap] or calico [muslin] have been stitched on to some of the edges. These are known as flies or flaps and are a technique used by some manufacturers as a means of saving cover fabric in places where it is not seen on the chair: on the seat at the sides and on the inside back below arm level and along the bottom. Do not take these sections apart when estimating the amount of new fabric required, but treat the section as a whole. There is no need to make flies on the new cover because the saving in fabric for an individual chair is small. Rip out

Left: *two typical easy chairs, one with squared, one with scrolled arms, can be given a new lease of life.*

any other sections of the cover which are seamed and iron out all the pieces so that they can be used as a pattern template for the new cover. Remove any calico [muslin] lining covering the foam and discard it.

The foam

If the chair has foam padding, examine it before removing it from the frame in case any of it can be re-used. Seat cushion foam will almost certainly have been compressed and reduced in thickness, as will the foam on top of the arms, and this should be replaced. The padding on the inside back of the chair and the inside arms generally remains in quite good condition and needs to be removed only if it is very thin and crumbling, or if the webbing or canvas beneath these pieces needs attention.

The springing

Most armchairs upholstered in foam have either tension springs or rubber webbing beneath the foam and these should be replaced if broken or flabby, following the methods on pp. 91 and 93. Some chairs have a spring unit—a set of coil tension springs joined by metal strips. Examine this carefully to see if it is broken in any way. If, for example, one of the clips connecting the springs to the metal strips has been broken, this can be replaced with a piece of wire. If the hole into which the clip is inserted has worn through, you can drill another hole and place the clip in that. If one of the springs has actually broken, it is often possible to replace it with a coil spring of a similar size. However, if the whole unit is badly damaged or rusty, it is not usually possible to replace it with a new unit, because it will have been made for that specific chair. In this case, the whole unit should be discarded and rubber webbing substituted, together with new rails to which it can be attached.

New rails

Make these from soft-wood, measuring 50×25 mm (2×1 in) by the inside measurement of the section of the seat frame to which they are to be attached. Using a 3 mm ($\frac{1}{8}$ in) bit, drill holes through the 50 mm (2 in) face of the wood at the centre and 25 mm (1 in) from the ends of both pieces. Screw the rails in position on the frame so that they will be level with the base of the seat cushion. The new webbing can be tacked to the tops of the rails.

Jute webbing

On some chairs, the foam on the arms and back is supported by jute webbing, which should be replaced, if torn, following the method described on p. 88. Hessian [burlap] covering the webbing and the front border should also be replaced.

Checking the frame

Before starting the new upholstery, check the frame carefully and make any repairs necessary.

You will need:
- Mallet and ripping chisel [tack remover]. Tack remover [nail-puller] or pliers
- Tack hammer and tacks
- Curved needle and twine
- Latex adhesive
- Paper, pencil, scissors for making pattern templates
- Foam for padding; wadding [padding] if necessary
- Calico [muslin] for inner covers, fixing foam to frame, etc.

1. *For scroll arms (chair on the left) the webbing is attached horizontally to give a firm foundation for the hessian [burlap] To form the correct shape, this is tacked to the arm tack bar, smoothed over the* arm and then tacked just below the scroll on the outside. On cap armed chairs (chair on the right) the webbing is tacked in vertical strands.

2. *For scroll arms, the rounded shape is formed by fixing the padding and cover fabric in one piece, following the line of the hessian [burlap]. The arm fronts are covered by separate*

- Piping or welting if necessary—that is, fabric and cord
- Webbing, jute or rubber if needed
- Springs if necessary
- Cover fabric

Foam

When replacing foam, buy the best quality you can afford in the correct density—that is, the load-bearing quality (see p. 88). Take the measurements from the chair frame for each piece of foam which needs replacing, making a paper template for any curved or shaped pieces. Allow 6mm ($\frac{1}{4}$in) all round each piece where you will be forming square edges and 25mm (1in) all round for rounded edges.

To judge the thickness of the foam required, measure the corresponding piece of old foam and round up the measurement to the nearest thickness available. As a general guide, seating cushions should be about 75mm (3in) thick and soft seat cushions 10cm (4in) thick. The padding for arms, however, varies from 25mm (1in) to 50mm (2in), according to the particular design of the chair being worked on.

Cover fabric

Like the foam, this should be the best you can afford. It must be of a quality upholstery grade to wear and clean well. If you particularly want a fabric which is not really an upholstery grade, such as some heavy linen union fabrics, it would be more sensible to tightly cover the chair with calico [muslin] and make a loose or slip cover, so that it can be easily removed for cleaning and repair. If you do decide to make a calico [muslin] cover, you do not need to line the foam as described below.

To calculate the amount of cover fabric needed for a tight-fitting cover, lay out the pieces of the old cover on the floor with the lengthwise grain running the same way on each piece. Arrange the pieces with about 75mm (3in) to spare all around each one, so that they fit into the width of the fabric—upholstery fabric is usually 120-128cm (48-54in) wide.

Calico [muslin]

Although this may not have been done on the original, the parts of the chair which are padded with foam should always be covered with calico [muslin] to help protect the foam and to give a better surface for the cover fabric. To calculate how much material you want, lay out the pieces of cover which went over the original foam to make up the available width of calico [muslin], which can be anything from 90-180cm (36-72in), and measure the yardage as for the main cover. You will also need additional strips for attaching the foam. Allow enough to cut 10cm (4in) wide strips to fit the outside edge of each foam section.

Piping cord

Piping or welting the edges or seams of the cover adds to the tailored look of the chair. It is essential if you are using patterned fabric, as this is usually impossible to match where the panels of the cover meet (see p. 92). If the old cover was piped, you can calculate the amount of new piping required by measuring the amount used before. If you are adding piping, measure the edges where you intend to place it and add extra for fitting. If you intend to make a loose cover for the chair, the calico cover underneath should not be piped.

shaped pieces of fabric, slip stitched in place. On cap arms, the squared shape is made by using two pieces of foam and making the cover with a piped welt as shown.

3. The backs and seats of both chairs are padded and covered in the same way. Note how the hessian [burlap] is left loose below the webbing until the cover fabric is pulled through and tacked to

the frame. Rubber webbing spans the seats, covered with a fabric platform; the top edge of the front border was back-tacked to the frame and pulled over the webbing.

The new upholstery

Start by cutting out the cover fabric and lining, using the old pieces of cover as patterns. Add 75 mm (3 in) all around each piece to allow for easy fitting. From the remaining cover fabric cut strips for the piping or welting casing, as detailed on p. 92. From the remaining calico [muslin], cut the 10 cm (4 in) wide strips for attaching the foam.

Preparing the foam

Glue the calico [muslin] strips to the foam, placing them along the side face if you want square edges, or along the front face if you want rounded edges; see p. 88 for details.

Attaching the new upholstery

After any re-springing has been done, it is usually easiest to complete the padding and covering of each section before beginning the next section. Start with the arms, then do the back, and finally the seat, applying the padding and cover following the pattern of the original upholstery. If you have a loose seat cushion with no padding attached below it, cover the front border after the arms. Where you have sections of fabric which are stitched together before they are attached to the frame, fit the pieces on the chair wrong side out, fitting and pinning closely. Keep the fabric smooth and taut, with the grain straight in both directions. Pencil around the pinned line, take off the fabric, machine stitch together, inserting piping or welting where needed. Make up a loose seat cushion cover as described on p. 95.

Platforms

On seats with loose seat cushions, the rubber webbing can be covered with a simple fabric seat cover called a platform. To prevent this fabric from tearing when the webbing expands during use, it is tacked to the frame along the front edge only and strips of elastic are attached to the back rail, so that it can be tied to the back seat rail. The loose side edges are hemmed and covered by strips of cover fabric which are tacked to the front, back and side edges. These strips give a finished look when the cushion is put in place on the seat. The front border can then be back-tacked along the front edge of the frame, taken under the front strand of webbing and then tacked in place. *Back-tacking:* place the raw edge of the fabric, right side down on to the edge of the chair so that the raw edge overlaps the chair by 25 mm (1 in) with the rest of the fabric wrong side up. Place a strip of cardboard 25 mm (1 in) wide over the raw edge of the fabric and secure it to the chair with a row of staples or tacks. Fold the fabric up, pulling it firmly over the card to make a clean edge. Turn under the remaining raw edges and slip or whip-stitch.

Lining capped arms

When lining capped arms, which will be tightly covered by fabric, cut the calico [muslin] to cover the inside and top of the arm only. Tack the edge of the material to the arm tack bar, smooth it up over the foam and tack the other edge to the outside arm frame. The side edge of the calico [muslin] can be tacked to the inside faces of the arms, or left loose.

Styles of arm

The arms of most easy [over-stuffed] chairs are of the styles known as scroll, padded or capped. *Scroll arms:* the fabric covering the inside arm is tacked to the frame along the tack rail and then pulled tightly over the padding on the top of the arm. It is tacked to the outside arm at the top and to the scroll on the front of the arms, where it is often pleated. The front panel of the arm is covered with a separate piece of fabric, which may either be slip or whip-stitched in position, or attached by a separate wood facing which is screwed on to the scroll. Piping or welting is often inserted into the join and may either be tacked to the frame or stitched in the seam line of the fabric. The outside arm is covered by a separate piece of fabric, which is usually back-tacked along the top edge, slip or whip-stitched along the side edges and tacked to the underside along the bottom edge. *Padded or capped arms:* the pieces of fabric for the inside and outside sections are stitched to a strip which covers the top and front of the arms before being attached to the chair frame. The seams are often piped. The bottom edges of the fabric are tacked to the frame and, on the outside back and front, covered by the edges of the adjoining panels which are slip or whip-stitched in position. These seams may be piped or welted.

Upholstery at Your Feet

In making this transformation from a box or beer crate to an elegant padded footstool, you will learn how to make a square edge with a piped or welted cover to give a tailored finish to your upholstery. You will also learn how to handle traditional upholstery materials at their simplest.

You will need:

- Wooden box: choose a sturdy box such as an old crate, with a firm base. The box is inverted, so that the base forms the top of the stool
- Sandpaper
- Tack hammer [nail puller] and lifter
- Tacks
- Regulator or skewer, see p. 91
- Needles: for making the bridle ties which hold the stuffing in place, you will need a spring needle. This is a heavy-duty needle, 13 cm (5 in) long, curved along its length so that it can be pulled in and out easily. For edge stitching, you will need a 25 cm (10 in) straight upholsterer's needle, which is pointed at both ends
- Twine: very strong, smooth string made from flax and hemp, which is used for making bridle ties around the edge of the seat
- Scrim or burlap: loosely woven material which is used for covering the first layer of stuffing
- Calico [muslin]: used for covering the second layer of stuffing
- Wadding [padding]: used over the calico [muslin], to give an extra-luxurious feel
- Stuffing: use horsehair or fibre or moss

Horsehair is the traditional stuff-ing, but because it is difficult and expensive to obtain today, it is often mixed with hoghair. Old hair mattresses can sometimes be bought cheaply at jumble sales or in junk shops. If you wash and tease the hair carefully it will return to its original life and springiness. Alternatively, use Algerian fibre. This comes from Algerian palm grass, and, provided it is teased out thoroughly, it makes a good inexpensive stuffing. For a small box, with about 75 mm (3 in) depth of padding you will need about 1 kg (2 lb 3 oz) of either type of stuffing.

This method of upholstery involves using traditional hair or fibre as the padding. Foam rubber could equally as well be used, but you will get experience in handling traditional materials on a small, manageable scale, which will stand you in good stead should you decide to tackle a larger piece of furniture in the traditional way.

Preparing the box

Smooth the outside of the wood if necessary with sandpaper. Then turn the box upside down, so that the base is uppermost, and chamfer the edges of the base at roughly 45° all around, with a rasp or smoothing file tool. This provides a ledge on to which the tacks can be driven and also helps to prevent the cover fabric from being chafed and worn on the corners.

Cut a piece of scrim [burlap] on the straight grain, to fit the top of the box, allowing 13 mm ($\frac{1}{2}$ in) margin on all edges. Turn under the edges, keeping the folds even with the weave of the fabric. Tack the fabric to the box, spacing the tacks about 50 mm (2 in) apart and 13 mm ($\frac{1}{2}$ in) from the edge.

Bridle ties

Traditional materials are held in place with bridle ties. To make these, thread the curved spring or mattress needle with enough stitching twine to go one and a half times around the stool. The stitch is like back stitch. Make a stitch in the scrim [burlap] about 25 mm (1 in) long and 25 mm (1 in) from the edge. Pull it through, leaving a 75 mm (3 in) tail. Tie the tail in a slip knot to the main length at the point where it emerges from the fabric. Working forwards, insert the needle 10 cm (4 in) away, pointing it backwards. Pull it out about 75 mm (3 in) from the starting point. Leave the stitch on top of the scrim [burlap] loose enough for your hand to be inserted easily. Continue around the edge in this way, making sure that a 25 mm (1 in) stitch falls at each corner. You may have to adjust the length of the bridles to do this. Finish off by tying a slip knot. Tease out a handful of stuffing and put it under one of the bridle ties, working the stuffing well together to prevent lumps. Do this for all the ties, then fill in the middle with more stuffing, teased out to make the shape even, letting it overhang the edge slightly by the same amount all round.

Covering the stuffing

Cut a piece of scrim [burlap] large enough to cover the stuffing to the chamfered edges all around with 13 mm ($\frac{1}{2}$ in) to spare. Place the fabric centrally over the stuffing, turn in the raw edge so it is level with the bottom of the chamfered edge, insert a temporary or stay-tack (one driven halfway in) to hold the scrim [burlap] in place. Smooth the fabric over the stuffing to the opposite side, turn under the raw edge so it is level with the bottom of the chamfered edge and place a temporary tack in the middle. Still keeping the weave of the fabric straight, smooth it out to the sides, turning under each edge, and tap in a temporary or stay-tack. Go back to the first edge and finish tacking it, driving the tacks into the chamfered edge and placing them about 25 mm (1 in) apart. Stop about 50 mm (2 in) from the corners. Complete other edges in the same way. To finish the corners, cut away the excess fabric at the bottom and tuck the remaining corner under the stuffing (see p. 112). Keeping the shape of the stuffing at the corners as square as possible, form any excess fabric into an inverted pleat by pinching the corners together. Tack down.

Regulating or easing the stuffing
During the covering process, you may have worked the stuffing out of shape, so use the regulator or skewer to even this out. Poke the sharp end of the needle through the fabric and ease the stuffing into a good, even shape. Keep feeling it and adjusting it until all is smooth. Only when you are completely satisfied should you begin stitching the edge.

Stitching the edge
This is done in two stages. The first, which is called blind stitching, pulls enough stuffing to the sides to enable a solid edge to be built up. The second stage, called top stitching, forms a roll from this section of stuffing. The roll must be really firm, because the cover fabric is pulled over it, and any unevenness will spoil the shape.

Blind stitching
Thread the upholsterer's needle with a good length of stitching twine. Then, starting at a corner and working along the side of the stool from left to right, insert the unthreaded end of the needle into the scrim [burlap] just above the tacks, 38 mm (1½ in) from the corner. Insert the needle into the

stuffing at an angle of about 45° to the horizontal and with the point offset to the left, so that it will emerge on the top of the stool about 25 mm (1 in) in from the edge and 13 mm (½ in) nearer the corner (point A). Pull the needle through, stopping as soon as you see the eye, so that it is not completely withdrawn. Push it back into the stuffing again, altering the angle so that it emerges through the side on the same level as it first entered, but 25 mm (1 in) nearer the corner (point B). You have, in effect, made a V-shaped stitch in the stuffing. Pull the twine through so that there is a tail about 75 mm (3 in) long left at point A. Tie it to the main length with a slip knot and pull tight. Insert needle 50 mm (2 in) further along the edge from point A, slanting it in the same way as before and bringing it out on the same level on top as the first stitch. Bring it down again at an angle to emerge about 25 mm (1 in) back. Before withdrawing the needle, wind the twine which is to the left of the needle around it twice anti-clockwise [counter-clockwise]. Pull the needle through completely. Put the unthreaded end of the needle into the centre of the stool top to anchor it temporarily. Hold the edge of the stuffing with your left hand, so that your fingers are on the top and your thumb is on the side; wrap the twine around your other hand and pull the stitch really tight, pressing down with your left hand at the same time.

Continue working around the edge in this way, being careful not to place the twisted section of a stitch so that it goes around a corner. To finish, knot the twine carefully and tightly. Correct any unevenness in the stuffing with the regulator, then re-thread the upholsterer's needle with a long length of twine.

Top stitching
This is similar to blind stitching, the main difference being that the needle is completely pulled through on top of the stuffing, so that a stitch can be made on the top. This means that the needle should be

inserted straight into the fabric and not inclined to the left, as with blind stitching. Starting at a corner, insert the needle 38 mm (1½ in) away, and 13 mm (½ in) above the blind stitching. Push it through to emerge on the top, about 25 mm (1 in) from the edge. Re-insert the threaded end of the needle about 25 mm (1 in) left of this point, keeping it parallel to the first entry, so that it emerges at point B, 25 mm (1 in) from point A. Tie the end of twine in a slip knot as before. Insert the needle again about 25 mm (1 in) to the right of point A. Complete the stitch, re-inserting it about 25 mm (1 in) to the left as before, just short of the first stitch. Before withdrawing the needle completely from the second half of the stitch, wind the twine around it and pull tight in the same way as for blind stitching. The stitches on top of the stool should form a continuous line, following the line of one thread of the fabric.

Second stuffing
Make more bridle ties round the edge and insert a second, thinner layer of stuffing under these over the scrim [burlap]. Take the stuffing right up to the roll and dome it slightly in the middle. This layer should be covered with calico [muslin] or scrim [burlap]. Cut it large enough to cover the top and come 25 mm (1 in) down on each side. Without turning under the edges, place it centrally over the stuffing and fix a temporary or stay-tack on each side, as for the scrim [burlap]. It should be quite smooth and tight. Tack completely along the edges to within 50 mm (2 in) of each corner, placing the tacks 25 mm (1 in) apart. Finish off the corners in a double pleat as for the dining chair (p. 88).

The cover: cut and stitch a cover to fit the four sides and the top as for the fireside chair seat cushion, see p. 95. Pull over the box, turn the raw edges inside the box underneath and tack in place.

Opposite: *for your first attempt at traditional upholstery techniques try this handy footstool.*

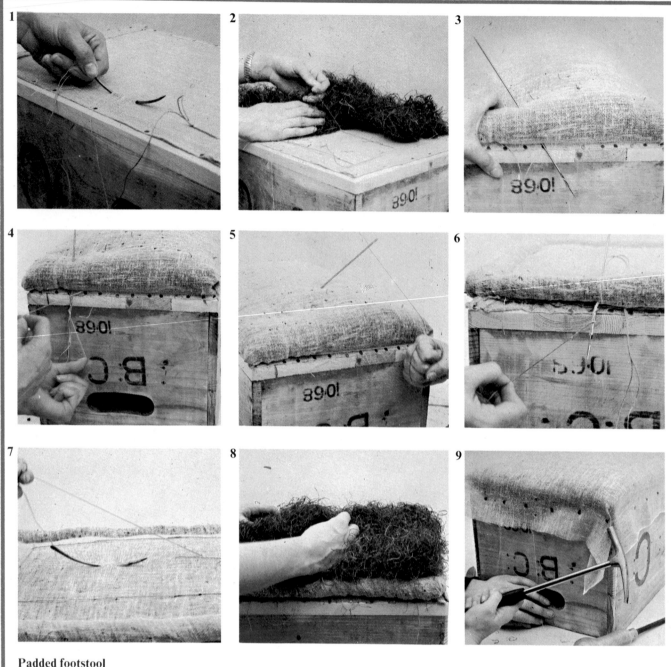

Padded footstool

1. *Make bridle ties of twine to secure the first stuffing. Tie the twine ends in a slip knot.*
2. *Tease out the stuffing before putting it under the ties.*
3. *Blind stitching makes a firm edge. Note the angle of the needle.*

4 and 5. *The second stage of blind stitching. Before the needle is withdrawn at the side, the twine is wound round it and pulled very tight.*
6. *Top stitch is a combination of back stitch and blind stitch and forms a roll of stuffing all round the edge.*

7 and 8. *Make more bridle ties for the second stuffing and fill the hollow left by the roll edge.*
9. *Cover the second stuffing with a piece of scrim [burlap], neaten or finish the corners, tack down and then make the top cover.*

Foam padding

If using foam (see p. 86), cut a piece large enough for the top and attach it to the box with calico [muslin] strips, as for the deep-buttoned bedhead on p. 120, using tacks or a staple gun. Cut an oblong piece of foam to cover all four sides of the box at once, and wrap it around, so that the foam covers the calico [muslin] strips and is level with the bottom edge of the box. Secure with adhesive or a few tacks.

Cut and machine stitch a tight calico [muslin] lining and pull firmly on to the box, stapling or tacking it to the box just above the open end. Make the cover from your chosen fabric, piping or welting the seams if you want a tailored look. Pull it on to the box, pull the raw edges over the open end and staple or tack them carefully inside the box.

Re-upholstering a Sprung Dining Chair Seat

Victorian dining chairs can sometimes be bought quite inexpensively from a junk shop and you can turn them into decorative and useful pieces of furniture simply by re-upholstering them in the traditional way with springs and horsehair. This also increases their value. Do not start by tackling a valuable antique—anything over 100 years old—that is a job for the experts.

You will need:

- Regulator or skewer. See p. 91
- Needles: for making the bridles which hold the stuffing in place, you will need a spring needle. For edge stitching, you will need a 25cm (10in) straight upholsterer's needle
- Twine [stitching twine or carpet thread]: this is used for making bridle ties, for stitching the springs in place, and for stitching the chair edges to make a firm edge
- Cord [spring twine]: a thicker twine, used for lashing the springs. Sisal may be used
- Scrim [burlap]: a loosely woven material used for covering the first layer of stuffing. Allow enough to cut a piece the size of the seat plus 15cm (6in) extra all round
- Calico [muslin]: used for covering the second layer of stuffing. You will need a piece the same size as the scrim [burlap]
- Wadding [padding]: this is used over the calico [muslin]. You will need a piece the same size as the scrim [burlap]
- Canvas [burlap]: choose a heavy furnishing variety. This is used to cover the springs, and you will need a piece the size of the seat,

plus about 25mm (1in) all around for edges
- Hessian [black cambric]: used to cover the underneath of the chair
- Coil springs: if it is necessary to replace damaged ones 12mm (gauge 10) wire ones, 10cm (4in) will probably be the most suitable. Or you can match the old springs
- Webbing: buy sufficient to replace the original webbing

Stripping off the old upholstery

The method has been fully described for the drop-in seat dining chair, see p. 86. As you work, make a note of the way the original top cover was attached, the number of springs and webbing strands, and the height of the original padding. Also note the size of tacks. If the chair seems a little too high or too low for your table, you will be able to adjust it with the new upholstery.

Examine the original stuffing carefully, if it contained horsehair—usually dark, very fine and curly—it is worth separating this from any wadding [padding], washing it and carefully teasing it out when dry.

Check that all the old tacks have been removed from the frame, however many there may be, to make room for the new tacks. If the chair has been re-upholstered before, you may find so many tack holes that it may be difficult to place the new ones securely. Fill the holes with plastic wood to give a firm base for your work. Repair the frame if necessary; treat for woodworm, making sure the frame is completely dry before you start work.

Replacing the webbing

The webbing, as before, is the basis for the rest of the upholstery, and so must be made taut and firm. The webbing is attached to the underside of the frame, as for the drop-in dining chair seat so you must turn your chair upside down on your work surface.

Attaching the springs

The springs must be sewn to the webbing and then lashed securely together at the top to prevent them from moving about in the seat. This lashing helps to give the seat a nicely rounded look.

Turn the chair the right way up and space the springs evenly in a square on top of the webbing intersections about 10cm (4in) apart. The curved tips of the springs should be turned to face the middle of the chair.

Thread the spring needle with a long length of spring twine. Using the fingers of your left hand (or right hand) to feel the positions from the underside of the chair, insert the needle into the webbing from underneath, so that it comes out level with the outside of one spring. Pull the needle through, leaving a short end of twine, and insert it into the webbing from the top, catching the bottom coil of the spring with a single stitch. Knot the end of the twine to the length pulled through, but do not cut it. Move to the other side of the bottom coil and, still with the needle on the underside of the chair, stitch it to the webbing. Make a third stitch, so that the bottom coil is held by three stitches, all in a V-shape.

Without cutting the twine, move to the next spring and repeat the process.

Stitch down all the springs in this way, with continuous twine, then make a slip knot to finish off, and cut the twine.

Lashing the springs

Attach two 13 mm ($\frac{1}{2}$ in) 'improved' tacks or brads on all four sides of the frame, each in line with a spring, hammering them halfway home. Cut off enough cord [spring twine] or sisal to stretch twice across the frame. Leaving an end which will stretch easily to the top of the nearest spring, plus a couple of inches for knotting, tie the sisal around a tack on the back rail of the chair and hammer the tack home.

Working towards the front of the chair, take the main length of sisal to the nearest spring and knot it to the coil which is second from the top on the outside. Take it through the coil to the other side and knot it to the top coil. Use clovehitch knots.

Move to the other spring in the row and knot the cord around the top coil on the nearest side, keeping the space between the springs the same as at the bottom. Take the cord through the spring and knot it around the coil which is second from the top on the front edge. Tie it tightly round the tack on the front chair rail and hammer the tack in.

Take the end of cord at each tack back to the nearest spring and tie it to the top coil on the outside, pulling tightly so that the spring inclines slightly towards the frame.

Repeat the process on the other pair of springs, with the cord running parallel to the first length, and then again with two lengths running across the chair. With careful adjustment, the springs will now give a rounded shape.

The main stuffing

The canvas [burlap]: centre the piece of canvas [burlap] over the springs. Fold over 25 mm (1 in) on one side of the canvas [burlap] and centre this on the back chair rail with the raw edge uppermost. Tack down with 13 mm ($\frac{1}{2}$ in) tacks, placing them 25 mm (1 in) apart and

13 mm ($\frac{1}{2}$ in) from the fold. To fit the inner cover at the back uprights of the chair, fold back the fabric corner diagonally so that the fold just touches the wood. Slash the fabric from the point to within 13 mm ($\frac{1}{2}$ in) of the fold. Trim off excess fabric and fold in raw edges level with the chair uprights. Tack the fabric down, pulling it as tightly as possible at the back corners. You may then have to adjust the other tacks.

Smooth the fabric over the springs, pulling it quite taut, and temporary or stay-tack, see p. 109, it to the front rail without folding, making sure the grain of the fabric is absolutely straight. Smooth, pull taut and temporary or stay-tack the fabric to the side rails. Check that all is smooth and straight grained, then hammer the tacks in completely. Trim off excess material to within 25 mm (1 in) of the tacks, then fold this over and tack it down at about 50 mm (2 in) intervals around the chair.

Stitch the springs to the canvas in a similar way, using continuous cord and a spring needle, but make a single knot at each stitch to lock it in position.

Bridle ties: see p. 101 for the bridle tie method.

Stuffing: take a handful of stuffing and tease it out thoroughly, removing any lumpy pieces. Put it under one of the bridle ties, working it well to prevent lumps. Do this at every bridle tie, then fill the middle with more stuffing, teasing it well to make an even shape and to overhang the edge slightly by the same amount all around.

Scrim [burlap]: place centrally over the stuffing and fix one temporary or stay-tack in the middle of each side to hold it in place. Put two other temporary or stay-tacks on either side of the central tack. At this stage the fabric should be rather loose on the surface of the stuffing. Thread an upholsterer's needle with a long piece of twine and stitch from the scrim [burlap] to the canvas in a rectangle about 75 mm (3 in) from the edges of the seat. To do this, pass the needle

Sprung dining chair seat
1. *The springs are arranged in a square on top of the webbing.*

2. *The base of each spring is sewn to the webbing with a spring needle and twine.*

3. *The springs are firmly lashed together with twine and then to the frame to prevent them moving about in the seat.*

4. *This is one way of winding the twine round the springs to hold them in place.*

5. *The springs are covered with a piece of canvas. The tops are then stitched to the canvas in the same way as the bases were attached to the webbing. Use the spring needle and a continuous length of twine and make a single knot at each stitch.*

6. *Bridle ties are stitched on the canvas to hold the stuffing material in place. Tease out the stuffing well and insert it under the bridle ties.*

7. *Anchor the stuffing in the middle of the chair by stitching through the scrim [burlap] cover to the canvas with the long needle and twine, being careful to avoid the springs.*

1

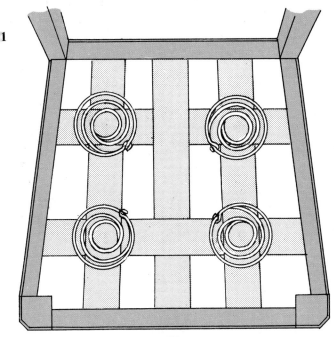

2

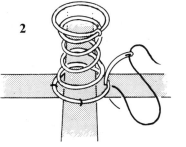

3

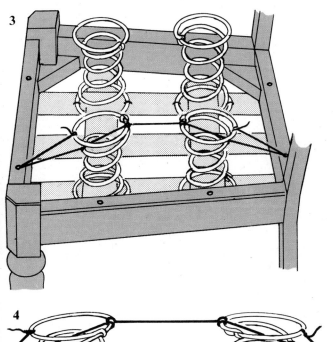

4

5

6

25mm
(1″)

75mm(3″)

10cm
(4″)

25mm
(1″)

75mm(3″)

7

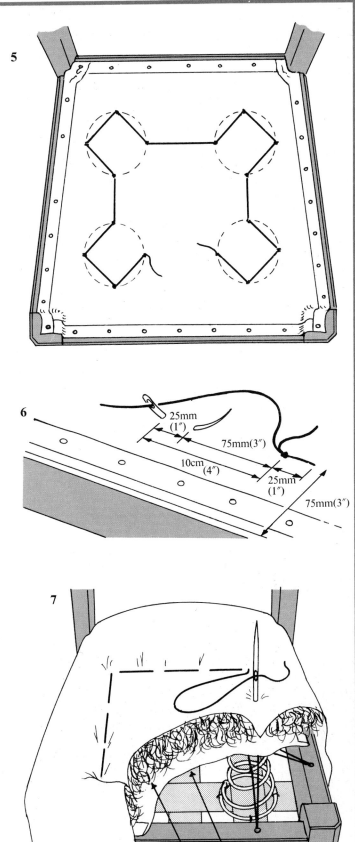

scrim [burlap]   stuffing   canvas

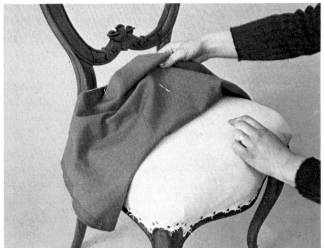

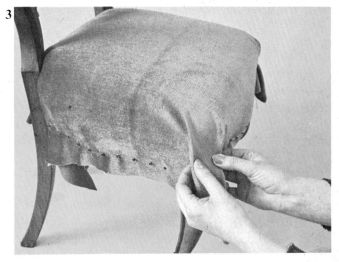

1. *Working top stitching round the edge of the chair to form a firm edge of stuffing to hold the shape of the seat. Work the stuffing and stitching as for the footstool in the previous section. Build up the rounded top of the seat with more stuffing.*

2. *When fitting the cover, be careful to keep the fabric grain straight down the centre of the chair. Mark both the seat and fabric centres, so that these can be matched.*

3. *Make sure that the fabric grain runs straight from side to side of the chair. Temporary or stay-tack in place to hold, and adjust if necessary before driving the tacks home. Make neat, matching pleats at the front corners and tack down when you are satisfied with the look. Cut and fit the back corners where the chair back joins the chair seat. Cover the line of tacks with upholstery braid for a neat finish.*

through the fabric and stuffing and pull it out between the webbing on the underside of the chair, leaving a tail of twine on top for tying off. As soon as the needle is completely through the canvas [burlap], keep the unthreaded end pointing down, and push the needle back through the material with the threaded end 13 mm ($\frac{1}{2}$ in) further on. Withdraw it on top and tie to the main length in a slip knot.

Push the needle back into the scrim [burlap] making a stitch about 75 mm (3 in) long on top. Continue round in this way, leaving a 13 mm ($\frac{1}{2}$ in) gap between the stitches.

Pull the twine tightly so that the scrim [burlap] is pulled down and be careful not to catch the springs as the needle passes through. Even out any lumps in the stuffing with the regulator or skewer. This process anchors the hair stuffing.

Remove the temporary or stay-tacks (holding the scrim [burlap] to the chair frame) from the front of the seat first, then the sides and lastly the back. Even out the horse-hair which is along the edges of the seat. Add more if necessary to make a fat roll which just protrudes beyond the edge of the frame. Tuck the raw edge of the material under the hair, smoothing it over the roll of stuffing. Use 10 mm ($\frac{3}{8}$ in) tacks to fix the folded edge of the scrim [burlap] to the chamfered edge of the chair frame. Do not pull it too tightly over the roll.

Stitching the edge: this is done in two stages following the instructions on p. 102. The first, which is called blind stitching, pulls enough stuffing to the edges to enable a firm edge to be built up. The second stage, called top stitching, forms a roll from this section of stuffing. The roll must be really firm because the cover fabric is pulled smoothly over it and any unevenness of shape would spoil the final result.

Start the stitching at the back, on the left side of the chair and work round the seat anti-clockwise [counter-clockwise], to include the back.

Continue working round the edge, being careful not to place the twisted part of the stitch so it has to go around a corner. To finish, knot the twine carefully and tightly.

Correct any unevenness in the stuffing with the regulator or skewer then re-thread the upholsterer's needle with a long length of twine.

Top stitching: this is similar to blind stitching, the main difference being that the needle is completely pulled through on top of the stuffing, so that a stitch can be made on top. See p. 102 for method.

Continue all round the edge in this way. The stitches on top of the chair should form a continuous line, following the line of the chair. *The second stuffing:* make bridle ties in the scrim [burlap], as with the first stuffing. Fill the depression in the chair seat which has been formed by the roll edge with more stuffing tucked under the bridle ties. Then cover the chair seat with a piece of calico [muslin], temporary or stay-tacking this with 10mm ($\frac{3}{8}$ in) fine tacks to the front of the frame, then the back and lastly the sides, keeping the grain straight. If the original upholstery finished on the sides of the chair rather than on the underside, be careful to place the tacks clear of the line where the wood begins to

show. Cut into the corners of the calico [muslin] at the back to fit around the uprights of the chair back. After the fabric has been positioned, hammer the tacks home, and tack along each edge.

If the front corners are rounded, make a double pleat or inverted pleat, and a single pleat if the corner is square. To keep a smooth line, pull the calico [muslin] firmly over the roll edges, but be careful to keep the fabric grain straight, by putting most of the pressure from back to front, rather than from side to side.

The top cover
To ensure a really smooth look, cover the calico [muslin] with wadding [padding] to prevent the

Above: *a hard-wearing velvet is the ideal material for these dining chairs.*

stuffing from working through. Then cut a piece of cover fabric on the straight grain, large enough to cover the seat, following the style of the original cover. Temporary or stay-tack with fine tacks through a single thickness. Finish the corners as for the calico [muslin] cover, and tack down. Trim off excess fabric.

Finishing
If the cover is attached to the edges of the chair where it shows, the raw edge and tacks can be hidden with braid or gimp, glued on with latex adhesive. Cover the underneath of the chair with hessian material [black cambric].

Forming a Roll Edge

In most cases, whatever your piece of furniture, small or large, the construction of traditional upholstery is the same: webbing, which spans the frame and supports the upholstery; springs (on larger pieces of furniture); hessian [burlap], which acts as a foundation for the stuffing; the cover. The method of application for all these materials can be adapted to suit your own piece of furniture.

The next stage of upholstery, however, may cause difficulties. It is the formation and stitching of the stuffing into the roll edge. This is an essential process in nearly all traditional upholstery, and it is one which requires practice.

Roll edges

These are made wherever the upholstery is 'over-stuffed'. This does not mean that there is too much stuffing, but where the stuffing is built up on the frame, so that the sides of the stuffing are at right angles to the frame rather than sloping away from it. Roll edges are made around seats of dining chairs, chaise longues and easy chairs, around the fronts of arms and around some backs of larger easy chairs. All these are places where the upholstery gets heavy wear. If the roll were not there, the top edge of the stuffing would not hold its shape, the surface would become lumpy and uncomfortable as the edge stuffing was pressed back, and the cover fabric would wrinkle.

When a roll edge is made by traditional upholstery methods, the stuffing is applied in two layers as described previously. The first layer

Right: *show off your upholstery skills with this over-stuffed, Victorian chair.*

is the main layer, using two or three times as much stuffing as the second layer. It is the first layer which is covered with scrim [burlap] and moulded and stitched into the roll edge. The second layer helps to form the final crown or domed shape of the padding. In some modern upholstery, the roll edge is made of foam rubber or by a manufactured roll of stuffing which is tacked to the edge of the frame, but neither of these gives as much wear as the traditional stitched roll.

Forming the roll

If you have already tried to make a roll edge, you have probably discovered that it was not difficult to make it firm, but that it took much more skill to form the stuffing into an even depth and into a shape which followed the line of the frame. The essential step in the process is the sight line.

Sight line: this is an imaginary line which lies along the edge of the stuffing where the horizontal surface becomes vertical. If these two surfaces met at right angles, for example, the sight line would be the angle. On a curved surface, the sight line lies in the centre of the curve. The sight line must be the same distance from the frame all along an edge and it should also be immediately above the line of the frame. If you were to stand above a chair looking down at a seat, the outside edge of the seat would be on the sight line, and this edge should also follow the line of the frame. It may also help you to follow the sight line if you draw a guideline on the scrim [burlap] before adding the stuffing. To do this, lay this material over the hessian [burlap] on the appropriate surface, matching the centre points of each side to those on the hessian [burlap] and temporary or stay-tack to hold it in place on the frame. Using a felt-tipped pen, draw round the edge of the frame on the material. Remove the scrim [burlap] from the frame and draw a second line outside the first, leaving a margin equal to the desired depth of stuffing, plus about 13 mm (½ in) for ease. Leave another margin of at

least 25 mm (1 in) outside the second line for turnings and trim off the excess scrim [burlap].

Applying the stuffing

It is essential to take time and care over applying the first layer of stuffing and attaching the scrim [burlap], because if this stage is well done, the stitching of the roll will be easy. Attach the webbing, springs, (if any), and hessian [burlap]. Work bridle ties into the hessian [burlap] – pp. 88, 101, 105 refer.

Chamfered edge: the scrim [burlap] covering the first layer of stuffing is always tacked to a chamfered edge—that is, a narrow angled surface between the top and side faces of the frame. This is because the tacks have to be put near the edge, and if they were not driven into the chamfered edge, they might split the wood. After stripping the old upholstery, check that the chamfered edge is strong enough to take more tacks. If there are many holes, fill with plastic wood and sand smooth when dry. If your chair does not have a chamfer, you can make one with a file. The edge should be at an angle of 45° to the top and sides of the frame and equal in width to the head size of an improved tack or brad. If your piece has 'horns'—a small raised section of wood at the front corners —also chamfer around these.

Shaping the stuffing: Insert the stuffing in the bridle ties (see p. 106) to the desired depth. Always make a note of the original stuffing depth before you strip off the old upholstery. Then, because the stuffing will probably have become compressed, cross-check the depth against any guiding features the frame may have. On the chair in the illustrations, for instance, the stuffing depth should equal the height from the seat frame to the tack bar at the back, and also from the seat frame to the show-wood at the sides. Compress the stuffing with the flat of your hand to gauge the right depth. Add the scrim [burlap], making sure that the centre marks are correctly aligned. Temporary or stay-tack the scrim [burlap] to the side face and work

the stitching, which holds the stuffing in place in the middle of the chair, as described on p. 106. Working on one side at a time remove the temporary or stay-tacks, lift up the scrim [burlap] and start moulding the stuffing into a roll of the desired size. It often helps to judge this by tucking under a roll of stuffing, smoothing it over and temporary or stay-tacking the second marked line to the chamfered edge. The scrim [burlap] should now be smooth but not tight.

Edge stitching

Blind stitching: work this as described on p. 102; the loop formed pulls the stuffing to the edge of the chair. On curved frames, take stitches of half the size to prevent marks on the scrim.

Top stitching: for each stitch, it helps if you form the roll between the fingers and thumb of the left hand. You can then insert the needle level with your thumb and bring it out on top of the stuffing, level with your fingers. Again, take small stitches, to prevent drag [pull] marks. The upholstery is now ready for the second layer of stuffing and for the covering.

Corners: pay particular attention to corners. For square corners at the front of a frame, pack in plenty of stuffing and fold the scrim [burlap] into a square pleat. At uprights, fold the fabric back diagonally and cut into the edge, just up to the fold. Pull the fabric down over the stuffing on each side of the upright and tuck in the pointed corner between the stuffing and the upright. Fold down the remainder in a neat square pleat. Check that the stuffing on each side of the upright is firm and not sloping away from the edge.

When you are satisfied with the shape of the roll, tack the scrim [burlap] to the chamfered edge. Make sure that the outer edges of the tack heads do not protrude over the edge of the chamfer or they will spoil the line of the final cover. Check that the line of the roll follows the frame exactly by tilting up the frame and looking at it from below. Adjust, if necessary.

Forming a roll edge

1. *Always make a note of the original stuffing depth before you strip off the old upholstery. Then, because the old stuffing may have been compressed, cross-check the depth against any guiding features the frame may have. In the picture, the chair's stuffing depth should equal the height from the seat frame to the tack bar at the back and also from the seat frame to the show-wood at the sides.*
2. *Making a chamfer with a file at the front corners to take tacks.*
3. *Folding the scrim [burlap] into a square pleat at the front corners. Note tack heads on chamfered edge.*
4. *Working blind stitch to pull stuffing to the edge.*
5. *Working the top stitch to form stuffing into a roll.*

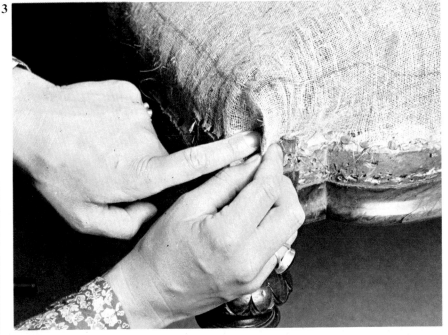

A Traditional Armchair Re-upholstered

It would take a professional upholsterer two to three days to strip down and rebuild a fully padded armchair by traditional methods, using the basic techniques of webbing, springing, stuffing and stitching. It will certainly take the beginner much longer. If you feel confident about the techniques already described, you can probably tackle this and other complicated upholstery with confidence. However, you must be prepared to allow plenty of time, working for short intervals over several weeks, if necessary, and without trying to do too much in one session. Therefore, try to find somewhere convenient to work where you will not have to clear up after each session. A spare room or garage is a far better workshop than the kitchen table which you may have used quite successfully for smaller projects. If possible, buy, make or borrow a pair of trestles on which the chair can stand. You can convert woodworking trestles by attaching narrow strips of wood round the top edge to prevent the chair from slipping off. You can, of course, work on a table, but the chair may keep slipping. Alternatively, you can work on the floor but this is tiring because much of the time you will have to spend at work on your knees.

Preparing the chair

Start by stripping off the old chair cover as described on p. 91. Remove any wadding [padding] and the undercover, if there is one. You can then examine the upholstery underneath. Look carefully at the webbing and hessian [burlap] supporting the stuffing on the arms and back.

Look at the fabric covering them. If the materials are torn and the stuffing is lumpy or falling out, they probably need replacement. Test the rigidity of any stitched roll edges: if these are flabby but still in good shape and the materials are sound, they can usually be repaired without being completely stripped. However, if the edge has completely fallen back, it is better to strip it off and replace. Tilt the chair so that you can examine the seat webbing and the springing from underneath. If the webbing is broken but the springing is sound, the webbing can easily be replaced from underneath without disturbing the rest of the seat. However, if the springs are out of shape or the cord lashing them together is broken, you should strip out the seat completely. If you feel that yours is a borderline case, it is much wiser to strip back to the frame, however tedious this may seem. With the cost of the cover fabric and the amount of painstaking work you will be putting into the job, it is essential that the inside of the chair is in good order. If you do decide to strip off the upholstery completely, remember to make notes and sketches at each stage about the number and positions of webbing strips, springs, the edges which are overstuffed (see p. 111) and stitched into rolls, the size of tacks, and so on.

Order of work

Generally, the best order of work is to complete the seat first, then the back, followed by the arms and finally the wings, if any. The re-upholstery of a traditional wing armchair is shown, which will probably be similar in many respects to your own, even if yours does not have wings.

One major difference, where you may have difficulties, is if your chair has an independent sprung edge. This is where the springs have been placed along the front edge of the frame, instead of a short distance back from it. The lashing of these front springs is done separately and in a different way from normal. If you have scroll arms, pad and stitch them as for seats.

The cover

The method of covering traditionally upholstered armchairs is very similar to that used for foam padded modern chairs described on p. 89. If you are simply re-covering the chair without renovating the upholstery, tease out the top stuffing on each section and add more if necessary. Add new wadding [padding] on the calico [muslin] cover. It is always worth applying a calico [muslin] undercover, even if this was not on the original, because this will help to shape the top stuffing and will give you practice in cutting and fitting a cover before you touch the more expensive upholstery fabric. The most usual mistakes made when fitting the cover are the incorrect alignment of the fabric grain, the incomplete pulling of the sections over the stuffing to make the cover smooth and taut, and inaccurate cutting around upright parts of the frame.

The grain must always be square to the frame, with the warp (threads running parallel to the selvedge [selvage] edges) running perpendicular to the floor at the centre of the relevant section of the cover,

although the grain may be pulled out of square at the edges where the stuffing tapers off.

Tautness is essential on each cover section and each piece must be pulled as smooth as possible without over-straining the fabric. To test whether you have pulled it taut enough, run the palm of your hand over the surface: there should

Above: *a traditional wing chair is a handsome, easy chair for a living room.*

be no wrinkles. If the fabric is not taut, it will crease when the chair is

115

Traditional armchair

1. *When replacing webbing where you are not removing springs, lay the strands between the springs for tightness. The springs can then be pushed inside the webbing.*
2. *Leave the back edge open when attaching the hessian [burlap] to the wings so that successive layers can be pulled through. The original stitched roll at the top has been re-used.*
3. *The original padding was removed in one piece for re-use. New scrim [burlap] and top stitching was worked along roll edges.*
4. *To enable the final cover to be pulled through, the back edge on the wings of the calico [muslin] cover was left open and the inside arm panel tacked to the outside face of the tack bar.*
5. *The final cover was applied over a layer of wadding [padding] for softness. To fit the fabric round the frame, the edge was folded back and cut in a 'Y' shape.*
6. *The fabric covering the inside arms was pulled through under the tack bar to prevent gaps between the arms and seat.*
7. *The fabric edge was clipped to give 'ease' for fitting the cover over the lower wings. The top was pulled firmly and evenly so no fullness was left on the front edge.*
8. *Top and front edges of the outside wing fabric were slip stitched. Back and bottom edges were tacked to the frame as the remaining panels covered them.*

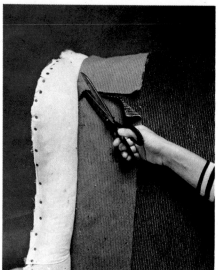
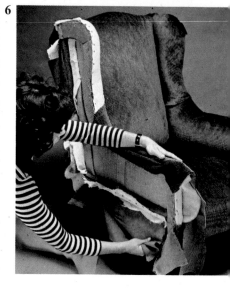
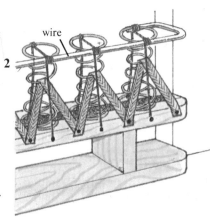
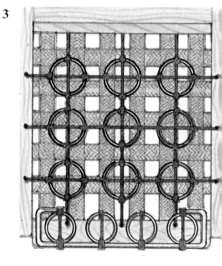

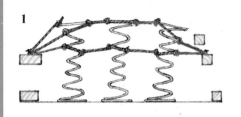

Independent sprung edges

1. *Two strands of lashing hold the middle rungs and the tops of the springs in place.*
2. *A strip of webbing is passed through the springs and tacked. This prevents squeaking when the springs are compressed.*
3. *A piece of cane or heavy wire is lashed along the front of the springs to make a firm edge.*
4. *Cord stitches pulled down to the front rail and tacked to hold the gutter in place.*

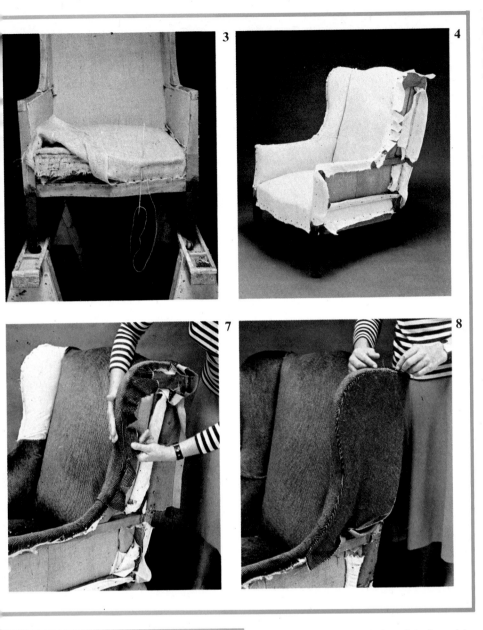

nere are 75-100mm (3-4in) lower and also softer than the other seat springs. Start by attaching the main seat springs in rows on the seat in the usual way (see p. 105). On some seats you may find it easier to make two strands of lashing across the rows, one tying the middle rungs of the springs and the other across the tops. Place the edge springs in position on the front rail. Use strong netting or electrical cable staples hammered in to fix them to the rail. Cut a strip of webbing to the length of the rail and pass it through the springs over the bottom rungs and tack it to the rail between the springs. This prevents the springs from squeaking when they are compressed and touch the rail. Cut a 15cm (6in) length of webbing in half lengthwise for each pair of edge springs. Tack one end of a strip to the left of the first spring on the front rail, pass the other end up and around the middle ring of the spring, pulling the spring forward slightly. Tack down to the right of the spring. Repeat for the remaining springs. To form a firm edge, a piece of cane or heavy wire is lashed along the top edge at the front of the springs. If you use a piece of wire, bend the ends to the shape as shown. Lash each front spring from the back at the bottom, over the top to the front edge.

Cut a piece of hessian [burlap] large enough to cover the top and front of the seat, plus 20cm (8in) for a gutter. The gutter is made behind the edge springs to allow them to move freely. The gutter is held down with cord stitches which are pulled down to the front rail and held with tacks between each spring. Tack hessian [burlap] in place and stitch to springs and wire. Apply the first stuffing, see p. 101, over the hessian [burlap], tucking plenty into the gutter. Apply the scrim [burlap] over the stuffing, making a roll at the front (see p. 111). Because of the edge springs, you cannot tack the edge of the roll to the frame; instead, stitch it to the hessian [burlap] with twine and a curved needle. Then stitch the edge into a roll in the usual way (see p. 112 for reference).

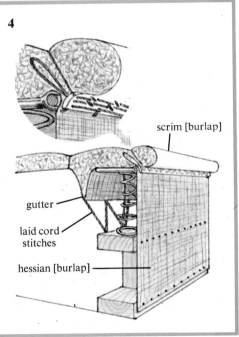

scrim [burlap]

gutter

laid cord stitches

hessian [burlap]

used. Always pull the fabric with the grain: if you pull with the bias it will stretch, and then sag.

Cutting

To fit the fabric around upright sections of the frame, turn it back so that the fold is level with the frame. Cut from the edge in a line which is at right angles to the fold and pointing to the centre of the upright to within 13mm ($\frac{1}{2}$in) of the fold. Then cut at an angle to each corner of the upright of the frame.

Independent sprung edges

These were devised to make the front edges of seats more comfortable. The front rail of the frame is higher than the remaining three rails of the seat and the springs used

Traditional Deep-Buttoned Upholstery

Deep buttoning is a decorative form of upholstery. It developed during the nineteenth century from the need to hold loose padding materials (horsehair and fibre) in place on vertical surfaces such as the backs of chairs and settees.

The cover fabric is pulled down deep into the padding at regular intervals over the surface and secured to the webbing with buttons which are tied on with twine. The padding is enclosed in the pockets thus formed.

The process causes a puckering of the fabric between the buttons which is neatened by folding the fabric into pleats. The pleats stay in place most easily when they lie on the bias grain of the fabric, so the most usual pattern of buttoning is based on a diamond shape.

For deep buttoning to look really good, the fabric must be smooth and taut with little puckering, and the mounds of padding between the buttons must be even in size and well rounded. This takes considerable skill when working with a loose padding material but is much easier with foam rubber—although, here, the technique is used for a purely decorative effect.

First we describe how to work deep buttoning with foam padding on a solid wood foundation, such as for a bed headboard: this is the easiest project to attempt while gaining practice in handling the fabric. Then we show how to develop the technique for traditional upholstery.

Deep-buttoned headboard
The foundation
This may be your old wooden headboard, a junk shop buy (check that it has the right fittings to attach to your bed), a new headboard cut from 13mm ($\frac{1}{2}$in) plywood or chipboard with a simple curved shape or a shaped unfinished ready-made headboard. It may have curved edges, but it should not be an intricate shape because you will not be able to achieve a smooth line with the padding.

The padding
Use polyether [polyurethane] foam in a low density, soft grade, cut in the same shape as the headboard but 25mm (1in) larger all around. Foam 75mm (3in) thick gives a luxurious look, but is harder to work with than 50mm (2in) or 65mm ($2\frac{1}{2}$in).

If the thickness of the padding would make the headboard so deep that the mattress would stick out at the end of the bed, leave an unpadded section, of the same depth as the mattress at the bottom of the board. The mattress can then slot in underneath. To check the exact point where the padding should end, put the unpadded headboard in position at the top of the bed. Fit the mattress against it and mark on the wood where the two meet. Leave an extra 13mm ($\frac{1}{2}$in) to give clearance and to allow for the thickness of the covering fabric.

The fabric
This is not the type of cover which can be removed for cleaning, so use a fabric which will not show the dirt quickly and which can be sponged or spray cleaned easily while it is still in position: a washable synthetic velvet is ideal. Any seams look ugly with this type of headboard, so if you are making one for a double bed—where standard 122cm (48in) furnishing fabric would be too narrow—choose a fabric which can be used sideways (with the selvedges [selvages] running horizontally, rather than vertically as usual). This means that you cannot use fabrics with a one-way design, although velvet looks all right with the pile running sideways.

You will need enough fabric to fit over the headboard and padding and around to the back, plus about 13mm ($\frac{1}{2}$in) in length and width for each row of buttoning. Allow about 23cm ($\frac{1}{4}$yd) extra fabric for covering the buttons. If you are leaving an unpadded section at the bottom of the board, you will need a straight strip of fabric to cover this. Allow the same amount of calico [muslin] for the lining, plus enough to cut 10cm (4in) wide strips to fit around the outside edge of the foam.

If you must join the fabric to make up the right width, this should not be done with a normal seam but by a special technique known as 'vandyking' (a special method of concealing fabric joins in the pleats of the deep buttoning) during the buttoning process.

You will need:
- Wooden bedhead
- Upholstery fabric
- Calico [muslin]
- Templates
- Foam
- Button moulds [forms] with 13mm ($\frac{1}{2}$in) diameter. It is wise to buy one or two more than the number you need in case you lose one. Have the buttons covered professionally if you prefer

Opposite: *learn the art of deep buttoning by turning an old headboard into an attractive addition to the bedroom.*

- One 13mm (½ in) improved tacks or brads for each button
- Tack hammer
- Several 10mm (⅜ in) fine tacks
- Staple gun and staples (optional)
- Twine: use nylon twine rather than traditional upholsterer's twine for extra strength
- Latex adhesive
- Drill and 3mm (⅛ in) drill bit
- Upholstery needle, 20cm (8 in) long
- Regulator or skewer (see p. 91)
- Rule, tailor's chalk
- Needle and thread (optional)

Making templates

After marking the height of the mattress, remove the headboard, place it on a large sheet of paper and draw round the edge of the wood. Cut out along the lines. Mark the height of the mattress on the paper and draw a line across it. Cut along this line. This template is the area of the board which will be padded and deep buttoned. The area below will simply be covered with fabric.

The buttoning pattern: to plan the positions of the buttons, mark the centre of each edge of the padding template. Draw lines across the template between these points on opposite edges. Working outwards from these lines, draw a grid with parallel vertical lines about 10cm (4 in) apart and horizontal lines 15cm (6 in) apart. Draw diagonal lines through the intersections to form diamonds of the required size. Mark the positions of the buttons at the angles of the diamonds. Leave a clear border without buttons of at least 50mm (2 in) all around the edge.

Fabric template: on a second piece of paper, about one and a half times the size of the padding template, make a pattern for the fabric by drawing a grid with the same number of lines, but spaced 30mm (1¼ in) further apart than on the padding template to allow for the fabric being pulled into the padding. Mark the button positions as for the padding template.

Working from the outside lines of the grid, mark the unbuttoned area to correspond with that on the

padding template. Then mark a second line, a minimum of 50mm (2 in) from this to give a margin for seams. Cut along this second line.

Transfer the markings of the button positions from the padding template to the back of the headboard. Drill a hole through the wood at each position. Place a temporary improved tack or brad below each hole on the back of the headboard.

Preparing the foam

Tear strips of calico [muslin] 10cm (4 in) wide to fit each side of the foam plus 25mm (1 in) to overlap at each corner. To fit shaped sides, cut several short lengths of calico [muslin]. Fold the strips in half lengthwise and apply the adhesive from the edge up to the crease line to within 25mm (1 in) of each end. Mark a border with a felt-tipped pen, 50mm (2 in) wide away from the edge of the foam on one side and apply adhesive from the edge to the line. When the adhesive is sticky, adhere the strips to the foam, keeping the crease line level with the edges. On the curved edges overlap the strips.

Attaching the foam: remove any struts from the back of the headboard. Place the foam on your work surface with the calico [muslin] strips downwards. Place the headboard front side down onto the foam, so that there is a 25mm (1 in) border of foam showing around the edges (or along the top and sides only if an unpadded section is being left at the base of the board). Squash up the edges of the foam so that they are level with the edges of the headboard; bring the strip at the top of the board over on to the back and secure with temporary or stay-tacks, placed at 15cm (6 in) intervals. Do the same at the sides and bottom. If you are leaving an unpadded section, tack the calico [muslin] on to the front of the board.

Beginning at the centre and working out to the sides, completely secure the top and bottom edges with staples, placing them about 20mm (¾ in) apart and about 6mm (¼ in) from the edge.

Release the temporary or stay-tacks as you complete each side. Ensure all the staples lie flat on the surface and tap them down lightly if necessary. To remove a staple, lever it up with a screwdriver or skewer and pull it out with pincers.

At the corners, slash the overlapping calico [muslin] level with the sides of the board to the corner of the wood and then to the front edge of the foam. Open the slashed portion out and refold it the other way so that it wraps around the sides and some extends at the corners. Tack it down and trim off the surplus material flush with the edges of the board. Tack and staple the side strips in the same way.

Main cover

Cut out the fabric using the fabric template. If you need to join the fabric by vandyking, read the section on this technique before you begin (see p. 123).

For the unpadded section at the bottom of the board, cut a rectangle of fabric to the required size, plus 10cm (4 in) all around. From the remaining upholstery fabric cut the required number of button moulds [forms]. Using the fabric template, mark the button positions on the fabric with either tailor's chalk or tailor's tacks. Work a tailor's tack by making a double stitch with double thread. Place the fabric on the foam so that the centre button positions are aligned.

Working on the centre diamond and starting at the back of the board, pass the needle eye first through the hole in the wood and out through the foam and fabric. Check that the needle is straight, and leave it with about 50mm (2 in) protruding. Thread about 50cm (20 in) twine through the shank of the button and then thread both ends of the twine through the eye of the needle. Pull the needle back through the board, unthread it and tie the twine in a slip knot below the tack. Tighten the knot and leave the ends hanging. Repeat this process for the remaining buttons of the centre diamond, using the flat end of the regulator or skewer to neaten

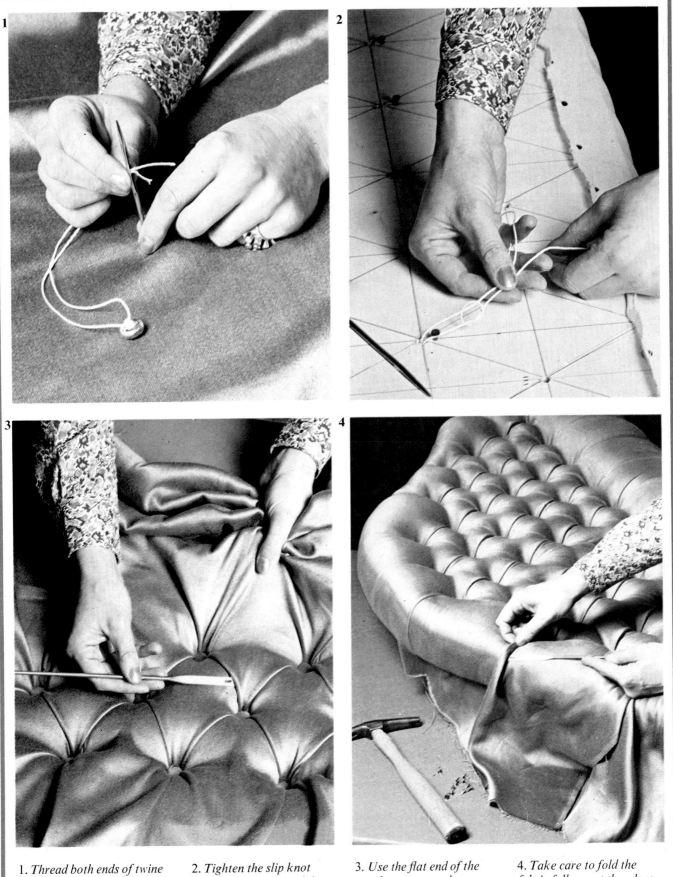

1. *Thread both ends of twine onto the needle through to the back of the board.*

2. *Tighten the slip knot round the tack behind the bedhead to pull down the button into the foam on the right side of the board.*

3. *Use the flat end of the regulator to ease the fullness between the buttons into pleats.*

4. *Take care to fold the fabric fullness at the edges of the bedhead into pleats.*

Above: a well-upholstered headboard.

the fullness that forms between the buttons into pleats. The exposed folds of pleats should face downwards. Continue working from the centre diamond outwards in this way, forming one complete diamond at a time. It is usually easiest to set the pleats and to keep the grain of fabric straight if you form each diamond before tightening the twine. When all the button positions are formed, neaten the fullness at the edges into pleats which lie at right angles to the edge so they face outwards from the centre top and downwards on the sides.

Smooth the edges of the fabric around to the back of the headboard at the top and sides. Be careful not to pull too tightly or you may lose the outside pleats. Where you have left an unpadded section at the bottom of the headboard, tack the bottom edge through the single thickness close to the bottom of the foam on headboard front. Tighten all the slip knots again and hammer down the tacks. Cover the unpadded section with fabric. If you wish to cover the back of the headboard, place a piece of upholstery wadding [padding] over it, cut a piece of fabric to size, plus a margin all around. Back-tack (see p. 100) the bottom edge to the board. Fold the fabric on to the board, pulling it firmly over the card to make a neat edge. Turn under the remaining three edges, snipping curves to make a smooth turned line. Pin in place, then slip stitch (see p. 94) the fold to the

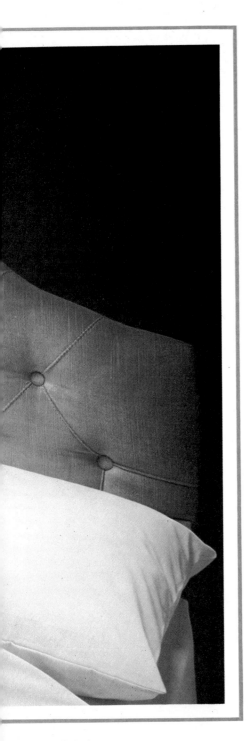

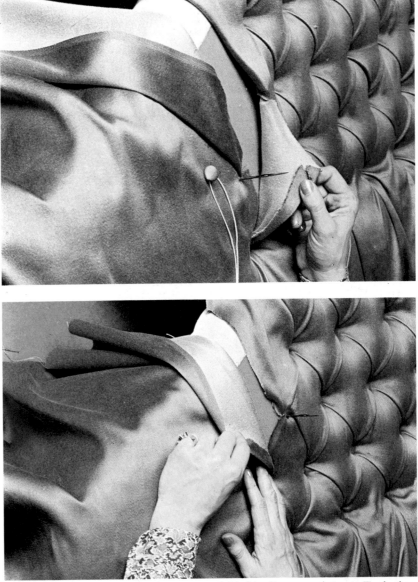

Vandyking is a method of making fabric joins in deep buttoning so that the join is invisible and un-sewn. Top picture: *The zigzag edge is clipped in each of its angles and folded in.* Bottom picture: *Tuck the raw edges under the folded edges to conceal the join. The buttons hold the fabric in place, when stitched with twine in the usual way.*

cover fabric.

Vandyking

In this method of joining the fabric, no sewing is actually done because the fabric is cut in a zigzag shape, so that the edges of the join can be concealed under the pleats of the diamonds and held in place by the button twine or twist.

Start buttoning with a full fabric width, working from the middle of the headboard out to the sides as previously described. When you reach the last row of buttons poss-ible with the width, form all the pleats but do not tighten the twine. Trim off the excess fabric at the sides to within 13 mm ($\frac{1}{2}$ in) of the pleats, following the zigzag line of the diamond shape. Leaving the pleats formed, remove the last row of buttons. Mark the button pattern on the new panel of fabric and lay it in place on the part still to be covered on one side of the head-board, so that the grain of fabric is absolutely square and the edge overlaps by 25 mm (1 in). Cut along this edge in a zigzag pattern to correspond with the first edge and clip into the angles for 13 mm ($\frac{1}{2}$ in).

Fold under the edges for 13 mm ($\frac{1}{2}$ in) on the sides which come at the top of each diamond on the second panel. Lay these *over* the top edge of the last diamonds formed in the main panel, so that the folds are quite level. Tuck the edges that come at the bottom of the diamonds on the new piece *under* the folds at the bottom of those in the main panel. Stitch down with twine in the normal way.

123

Deep buttoning a chair

When you have successfully re-upholstered a dining chair by traditional methods, and have done some deep buttoning with foam padding, you could combine the techniques on a traditionally upholstered or over-stuffed chair which has a deep-buttoned seat or back. The method for working the deep buttoning on this furniture is very similar if the back is of an 'over-stuffed', (see p. 111), style—where the stuffing is built up on the frame and the covering fabric is taken over the whole surface and tacked to the outside back. The method is different, however, on backs which have shallower, inset padding surrounded with a decorative border of wood.

You will need:

- Mallet and ripping chisel [tack remover]
- Webbing and webbing stretcher
- Hessian, scrim [burlap], upholstery wadding [padding]
- Horsehair stuffing
- Twine
- Calico [muslin], upholstery fabric
- Button moulds [forms]
- Spring needle [curved upholstery needle]
- Double-pointed straight needle
- Improved and fine tacks or brads; tack hammer
- Regulator or skewer, see p. 91, scissors
- Tailor's chalk
- Braid for trim and adhesive for applying it—chairs with show-wood only

The stuffing

In order to keep the cover fabric smooth between buttons, the stuffing must be well packed, which tends to make the surface rather hard. This can be modified by using a good quality horsehair stuffing, which has a lot of springiness even when firmly packed. Good quality horsehair has long lengths of hair—15-20 cm (6-8 in) long—in comparison with the shorter lengths of cheaper hair. You may find that your original stuffing was good horsehair, in which case it is

worth re-using it. You can restore its springiness by washing it in mild soapy water, rinsing it well and drying it in a warm place.

The fabric

Traditionally, button-back chairs were covered in leather or velvet. Of the two, velvet is the easier to work, because it will form into pleats naturally under the pressure of your hand, whereas leather has to be hammmered down and is really a job for a professional. The original cover will give a guide as to the amount you need, although it is advisable to allow an extra 15 cm (6 in) all around to give some leeway, particulary if you are adding more stuffing. You will need the same amount of calico [muslin] for the inner cover. The buttons are covered in matching fabric, and you can make them yourself by covering metal moulds [forms], or you can have them done professionally.

Backs and unsprung seats

Strip off the old upholstery fabric, and, if the original surface was deep buttoned, keep it as a guide to the amount of new fabric required.

Examine the upholstery underneath to see whether it needs replacing: if the hessian [burlap] is in good condition and the scrim [burlap] is not torn, you may simply need to wash and tease out the second layer of horsehair stuffing and add more if necessary. Then replace the calico [muslin] and cover as described below. If the upholstery does need replacing, proceed as follows.

Strip off the old upholstery, see p. 91. Keep the scrim [burlap] covering the first stuffing as a guide to the buttoning pattern. Start the new upholstery as described for sprung dining chairs (p. 105) and work the blind and top stitching as previously described, see p. 102. If you are working on a back, follow the same principles, using the original upholstery as a guide to the details.

Right: *a balloon-backed, deep-buttoned, Victorian dining chair.*

The buttoning pattern: make a template of the surface to be covered by holding a piece of paper over it and drawing around the edge. Find the centre point of each edge and draw lines across the template between the centre points on opposite edges. If the original surface was buttoned, measure the distance between the rows of buttons on the scrim [burlap] (saved from the stripped upholstery) and draw a grid on the template to correspond. If the old surface was not buttoned, start from the centre lines and draw a grid of parallel lines as for the bedhead, see p. 120. Make the positions for the buttons to form diamond shapes, leaving a clear border of about 50mm (2in) all around.

Fabric template: make a second template for the upholstery fabric, with the lines 38mm (1½in) further apart as described for the bedhead. Remember to allow extra all around for the unbuttoned border and for the depth of the padding. Use the template as a guide to the amount of calico [muslin] and cover fabric required.

The second stuffing: using tailor's chalk or ball-point pen, transfer the markings from the buttoning template to the scrim [burlap] covering the first stuffing. To make holes for buttons to sink into the stuffing, cut a slit in the material at each button position and insert your index finger into the stuffing until you can feel the hessian [burlap] below (see picture 1). To make markers so you can find the button positions when the second stuffing is in position, thread the long needle with about 30cm (12in) of twine, pass it through the hole

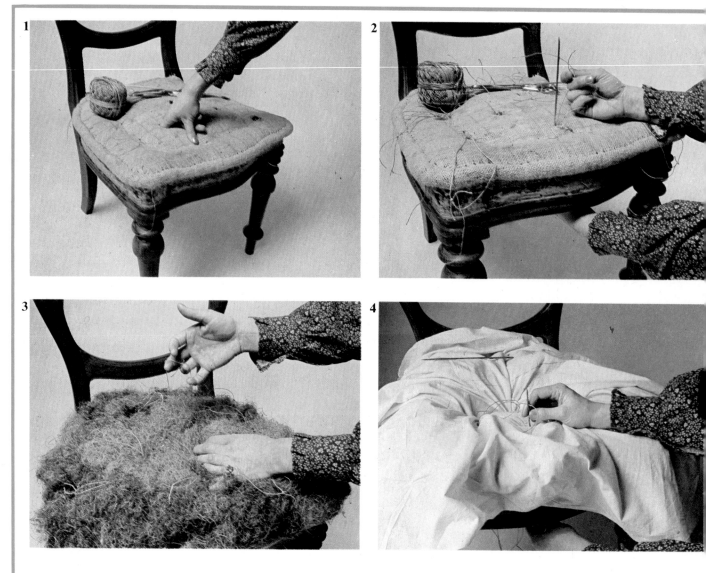

Deep button chair

1. At each button position insert an index finger into the stuffing through the hole in the scrim [burlap] to ensure the buttons sink deeply into the seat.

2. Making twine markers for each button position. The needle is passed through the stuffing to make a small stitch in the hessian [burlap] below, before being pushed back.

3. When the second stuffing is added, the twine markers are pulled through it to indicate button positions.

4. Pass the needle through the calico [muslin] and stuffing to the underside of the chair. The tail of twine on top is treated in the same way after making a small stitch.

and stuffing and pull out underneath. Make a small stitch in the hessian [burlap] and then push the needle back. Tie the ends of twine together. Repeat for each button position. Make bridle ties (see p. 101) for the second stuffing. Pull the markers through it.

Calico [muslin] cover: you may feel tempted to rush over this stage in your eagerness to see the effect of the main cover. But, in fact, this is one of the most important stages in the buttoning processes, because it shapes the second stuffing into the mounds between the buttons, so

take time and be patient. Transfer the markings of the button positions from the fabric template to the calico [muslin] cover with tailor's chalk or tailor's tacks. Place the calico [muslin] cover over the second stuffing and align the centre button positions. Press the material down into the stuffing and into the holes in the scrim [burlap]. Start at the centre button and work each diamond in turn. For each button, thread the straight upholstery needle with 30 cm (12 in) of twine. Insert the needle into the calico [muslin], through the hole

and bring it out on the reverse side (that is, the underside of a seat or the outside back of a chair). Pull through leaving a tail of twine about 15 cm (6 in) long on the calico [muslin]. Unthread the needle and re-thread it with the 15 cm (6 in) tail. Insert the needle into the calico [muslin] again, making a stitch of about 6 mm ($\frac{1}{4}$ in). Pull through and unthread the needle. Tie the ends of twine on the reverse side in a slip knot and tighten the knot around a small roll made from a scrap of material to prevent the knot pulling back through the stuffing.

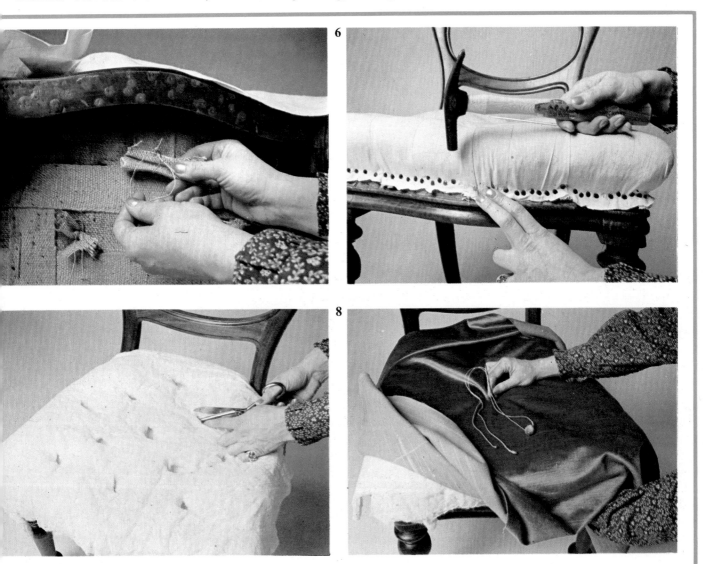

5. *Tightening the twine in a slip knot around a roll of scrim [burlap] under the chair.*

6. *Tacking down the calico [muslin,] placing the tacks above the cover's tack line. Notice how the fullness at the edge is formed into pleats on the straight grain.*

7. *Making slits in the wadding [padding] at each button position, so the cover buttons can be pulled down firmly. The wadding [padding] prevents any horsehair from working through.*

8. *Attaching the cover fabric. The button is threaded on the twine first, so that both ends of twine can be threaded in the needle and passed through the stuffing together.*

127

Above: tackle a Victorian chair the easy way; deep button the back, but leave the seat plain.

Repeat this process at the remaining button positions, neatening the fullness that forms between the stitches into pleats. On the backs of chairs the pleats should face downwards; on seats they should face the front edge. Feel the mound of stuffing in the diamond; it should be firm and smooth. If it is flabby, poke some more stuffing into it with the flat end of the regulator or skewer and prod it with the pointed end until the shape is correct. If the calico [muslin] seems taut, you are likely to have trouble keeping the grain straight when you work the adjoining diamonds. It may be because there

is too much stuffing, in which case you should use the regulator or skewer to hook some out. Continue working in this way, completing each diamond at a time. Neaten the fullness at the edges into pleats which lie on the straight grain and tack down the calico [muslin] to the seat, placing the tacks just above the tack line of the original cover.

Main cover
Mark the wrong side of the cover fabric in the same way as for the calico [muslin]. Use the remaining scraps of fabric to cover the buttons. Cut a piece of wadding [padding] to cover the calico [muslin] and place it, 'skin' side out, in position. Make a slit in the wadding [padding] at each button position. But do not press it down

into the holes. There is no need to tack the wadding [padding] in position. Put the cover fabric in place and start buttoning, as for the calico [muslin]. This time, thread a button on the twine first, so that both ends of twine can be threaded in the needle and passed through the fabric together (picture 8). Knot and tighten the slip knot around the same hessian [burlap] roll as for the knots on the calico [muslin]. Continue buttoning, keeping the grain of the fabric absolutely square. Tack the cover to the frame along the tack lines of the original cover and trim off the excess fabric. Finish with braid or gimp if desired. Use adhesive or gimp tacks to secure.

Sprung seats
These are deep buttoned in a similar way to unsprung seats, except that the twine is tied on the right side instead of the reverse side because of the springs. To make the stitch, insert the needle from the right side, leaving a tail of twine. As soon as the needle's eye is through the hessian [burlap] above the springs, push it back, eye first, making a small stitch on the reverse side of the hessian [burlap]. Insert the small roll of hessian or scrim [burlap] into the stitch on the reverse side (this process may seem fiddly at first, but you soon get the knack). Tie the ends of twine on the right side into a slip knot, threading the button on to one end of the second length used at the main cover stage. Pull the knot tightly. When all the button positions are stitched, cut the ends of twine, leaving about 13 mm ($\frac{1}{2}$ in) on the length used at the calico [muslin] stage, but only 6 mm ($\frac{1}{4}$ in) on the length used on the main cover. Tuck the ends under the buttons. Cut a piece of fabric for the outside back panel, if buttoning the back of a chair, and tack it to the frame. Trim the excess fabric to be level with the tacks, and cover with braid or gimp. If the front cover fabric is pulled over and tacked to the back of the frame, the raw edges will be covered by the back panel, which is slip stitched, (see p. 94), in place.

Chair Backs and Padded Surfaces

Traditionally upholstered chair backs vary in style from light padding on dining chairs to thicker padding and deep buttoning on larger easy chairs.

When the upholstery consists of padding built up on the frame, the techniques are similar to those used for seating. Some different techniques are used when the upholstery is inset with a border of wood showing around the edges.

Special equipment

To prevent the wood from being damaged, it is best to use a ripping chisel [tack remover] with a cranked shaft (from upholsterer's tool suppliers) for removing the tacks of the old upholstery. You will need a hammer with a fine head, for tacking down the new upholstery. For chairs and backs with thick padding you will need a curved needle for the blind and top stitching processes, because a straight needle would hit the wood.

To prevent damage to the wood:
- Place a pad under any sections which touch your work surface.
- Place a wood block (or mallet head) under tack rails as extra support when hammering in tacks.
- Allow a clear margin of 5mm ($\frac{1}{4}$in) between the edges of the webbing, scrim and hessian [burlap] and the wood, so that there is room for the tacks which hold the cover
- Try to avoid using the web strainer or stretcher against the wood. Or place a soft pad between it and the wood.

Light padding

Replace webbing, attach hessian [burlap], work bridle ties, insert stuffing, add wadding [padding], calico [muslin] and cover as before (see pp. 88, 101, 106), carefully trimming off the excess material with a handyman's knife so that all edges are inside the show-wood. Glue on braid or gimp, placing its outer edge just inside the show-wood.

Instead of horsehair, linter's felt [upholsterer's felt] (a thick wadding [padding]) can be trimmed to size and tacked firmly in place for light padding.

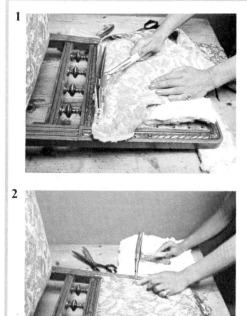

Far left: *Many pretty period-type chairs have panels of lightly-padded fabric set in show-wood panels in their backs. With a little extra care and a delicate touch with the hammer, these can be satisfactorily re-padded and re-covered.*

Padded chair back
1. *A layer of linter's felt was cut to size and used to make a barely padded back panel in this chair. Just the right amount of padding will be needed to give the right look. Use a hammer with a fine head to put the tacks in place, to avoid damaging the wood around the panel.*
2. *Trim off the fabric edges carefully, so the edges are inside the show-wood and add upholsterer's braid to cover the raw edges and tacks.*

Renovating a Chaise Longue

The chaise longue, meaning in French a long chair, was a popular piece of furniture in the nineteenth and early twentieth centuries. Although there are many variations in design, its components are essentially the same: an elongated seat on which people could lie at full length, a heavily padded head rest at one end, and a shaped back which usually has inset padding with show-wood. On all designs the construction of the upholstery is the same, and is also similar to that previously described. The major differences are detailed here, together with the different ways of attaching the cover. A slightly different way of deep buttoning is also introduced. Although quicker to do than the method previously described, its success depends on absolute accuracy in the marking of the buttoning pattern on the cover, plus allowances for pleating.

You will need:
- Mallet and ripping chisel [tack remover]
- Claw or Warrington hammer
- Webbing strainer or stretcher, if re-webbing seat
- Heavy duty scissors
- Curved upholstery needle
- Heavy straight needle
- Light straight needle
- Small curved needle
- Regulator or skewer (see p. 91)
- Upholstery materials
- Webbing, if necessary
- Tacks
- Scrim [burlap]
- Hessian [burlap and black cambric]
- Calico [muslin]
- Stuffing
- Twine
- Linter's [upholsterer's] felt

Order of work
Start by removing the old coverings and checking the original upholstery, to see what will need replacing. When applying the new upholstery, work on the head rest first, then the back (which you may find is removeable which makes the upholstery easier to fit) and finally the seat.

The head rest
If you had to strip this down to the frame, apply new webbing (see pp. 88, 101), following the original pattern. Cover this with hessian [burlap].

Bridle ties
These are worked with a curved needle and twine across the hessian [burlap] in rows about 15 cm (6 in) apart, see p. 101. Attach the twine to the edge of the hessian [burlap] and make a back stitch in the centre of the head rest, leaving a loop loose enough to insert two fingers. Tie off on the opposite edge, leaving a loop of the same size.

First stuffing
Insert the stuffing into the bridle ties, making it about 10 cm (4 in) deep, uncompressed. Allow the stuffing to overhang the front edge only. Cover the stuffing with scrim [burlap] and stitch through from the scrim to the hessian [second and first burlap] as described in the instructions for re-upholstering a sprung dining chair seat (see p. 106). Tack down the scrim [second burlap], making a firm roll (see p. 112) along the front edge which overhangs the frame by about 20 mm ($\frac{3}{4}$ in). When turning corners under, at the top, keep a slight diagonal pull on the material to

help shape it around the scroll. Work a row of blind stitch (for instructions see p. 102) along the front, back and the top edges, keeping it just above the tack line. Top stitch (see p. 102) the front edge only, making the roll about 38 mm (1$\frac{1}{2}$ in) high.

Second stuffing
Work bridle ties as before into the scrim [burlap] in the same pattern as before and apply the stuffing. Build it up to produce a crowned shape about 60 mm (2$\frac{1}{4}$ in) uncompressed in the centre, and feathering out to the edges.

Calico [muslin] cover
Cover the stuffing with calico [muslin] see p. 114, temporary or stay-tacking it to the underside of the top rail first. Smooth it down to the bottom, take it around the tack rail and temporary or stay-tack in position. Cut the calico [muslin] to fit around the upright and temporary or stay-tack in place. Strain the material over the top corners with a diagonal pull and temporary or stay-tack. Do the same with the front and back from the bottom to top. Tighten the bottom and top edges if necessary, drive in all the tacks and trim off the excess calico [muslin].

Top cover
If the top cover is to be plain, or shallow buttoned without a border, apply the upholstery fabric as for the calico [muslin] cover. If you are including a border, read the section on finishing styles, see p. 133, before cutting out.

Deep buttoning
If you are deep buttoning the cover,

130

proceed as follows. Following the pattern on the original cover, mark out the positions for the buttons on the calico [muslin]. If you prefer small diamonds as a pattern, mark the pattern. Using large sharp scissors, cut a diagonal slash, then make a 25 mm (1 in) diameter hole for each button through both layers of stuffing down to the hessian [burlap]. Make a button marker through each hole, as shown on pp. 126-127. Place a layer of felt or wadding [padding] over the calico [muslin], make a small hole at each button position and pull the markers through. Mark the buttoning pattern on the wrong side of the top cover with allowances for

Below: *A Victorian chaise longue deftly restored to its former glory.*

pleating and place it over the felt or wadding [padding].

Buttoning

Starting with the bottom row, pull the button markers through the fabric at the corresponding button positions. Thread a button on each marker and tie with a slip knot. Tighten the knot to pull down the button until the fullness of fabric has been taken up. Repeat this process for the next row of buttons and neaten the fullness between the buttons into diagonal pleats with the regulator or skewer as described on p. 120. Ease any fullness along the edges into pleats which lie at right angles to the edge of the frame and tack or sew down.

The border: if you are applying a border as a means of saving fabric

in the main panel, take the measurements for the main panel after the second stuffing and calico [muslin] have been attached. Measure from 25 mm (1 in) beyond the tack line of the back edge to just below the roll edge at the front. After working any deep buttoning (pp. 120-122), attach the back edge of the cover with tacks in the usual way, smooth the fabric to the front, and pin it to the stuffing just below the roll. Stitch in position with a curved needle and twine. Cut out the border to the appropriate size plus 25 mm (1 in) all round for fitting. Pin it in position along the roll edge where it joins the main panel of fabric and mark the fitting line on the border with chalk. Unpin and stitch piping or welting along the fitting line. Fold under

Chaise longue

1. Bridle ties which hold the stuffing in place should be worked in horizontal rows. You will need to insert more stuffing at the front edge to help build up the roll edge there.

2. After the first stuffing, cover the back with scrim [burlap], and tack the front edge firmly to make a substantial roll which overhangs the frame. At the top, a slight diagonal pull on the scrim [burlap] helps to mould the shape round the scroll.

3. Mark the buttoning pattern on the wrong side of the piece of cover fabric with allowances for pleating as shown.

4. Here is one method of marking the buttoning pattern, which works well if you like the look of small diamonds. Alternatively you can use the button positions on the original cover.

5. Add the border, with a piped edge if preferred, stitching it in place with a curved needle.

1

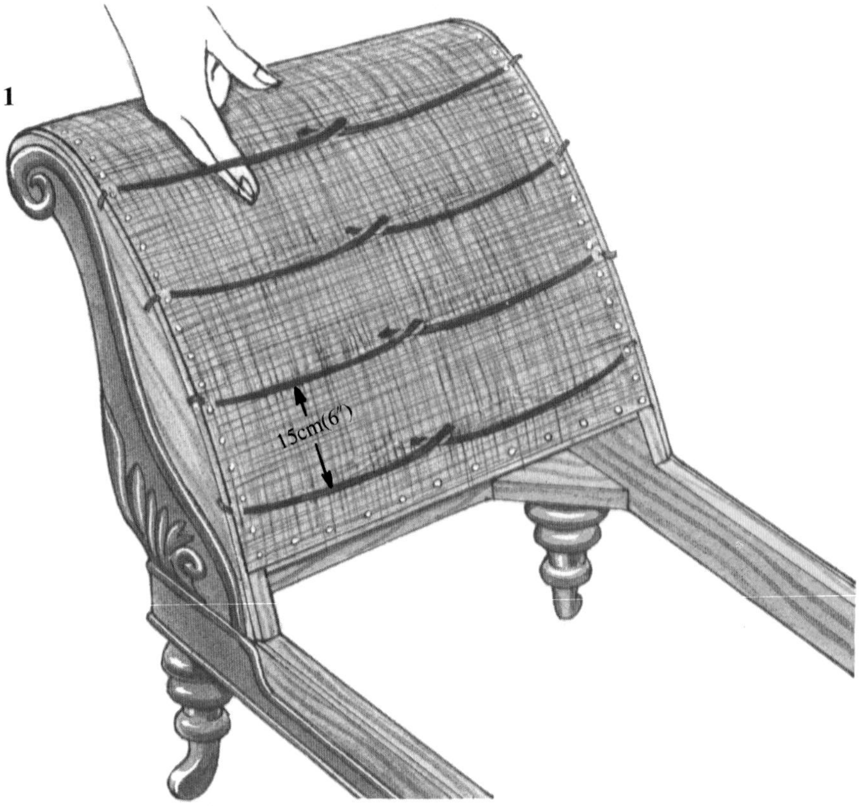

15cm(6″)

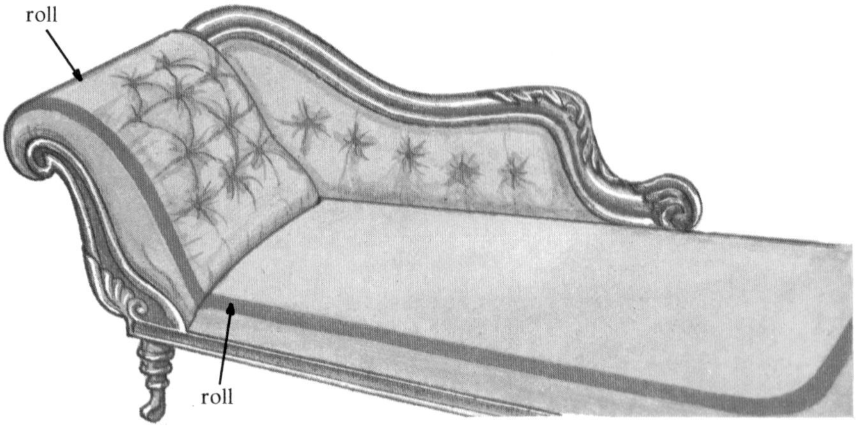

roll

roll

Right: *Indicated on the chaise longue drawing are the places where rolled edges are generally built up on the frame. You will need some practice in deep buttoning before you tackle a piece like this one.*

the margin along the fitting line. Re-pin the border in position and slip stitch, see p. 94. Tack the remaining edges.

The back: the back is built up and covered in the same way as the head rest. When applying the first filling, keep any edges which will be hidden flat, so that the back will fit tightly against the head rest and seat. Work blind and top stitch (see p. 102), along the top edge only.

The seat: the seat is worked in the same way as a dining chair (see p. 106). Make the first stuffing about 13 cm (5 in) deep, uncompressed, and allow it to overhang the front edge. Work the blind and top stitch along the front and bottom only. Border: If the cover fabric is applied with a border, stitch the main panel fabric just under the roll with a curved needle and twine. Cut the border and apply in the same way as the arm. *Finishing:* cut a piece of fabric to

cover the outside section of the head rest and apply it as for the outside back panel of an easy chair, see p. 94. On some styles, the back edge of this panel may be pulled around to the back and tacked there where it will be eventually covered by the back section.

Cover any raw edges with gimp or braid. Re-fit the back section to the chaise. Cover the works on the underside of the seat with a piece of hessian [black cambric], edges

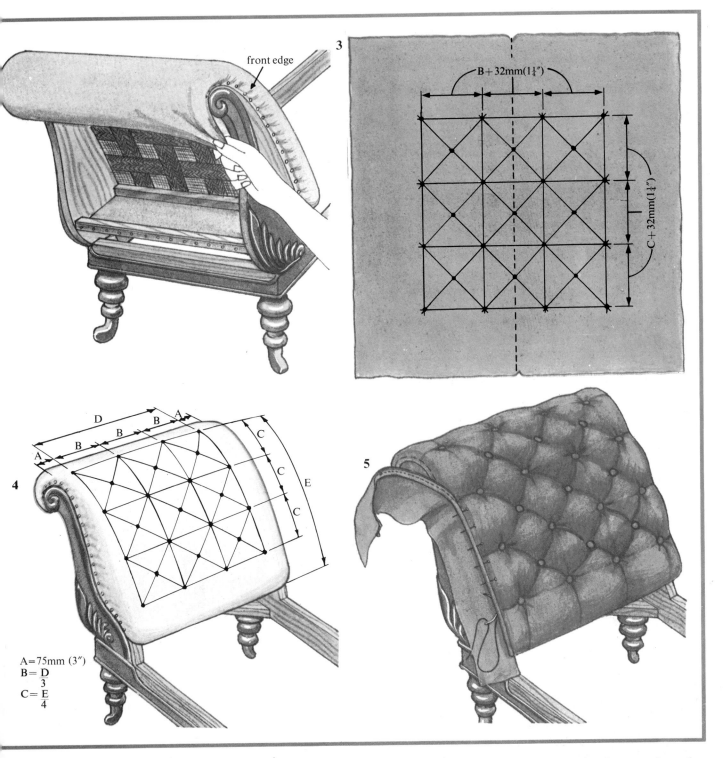

3

B+32mm(1¼")

C+32mm(1¼")

front edge

4

D B A
B B
A

C
C
E
C

A=75mm (3")
B=$\dfrac{D}{3}$
C=$\dfrac{E}{4}$

5

turned in and tacked all around.

Styles of finishing

There are three major styles of applying the upholstery fabric to the head rest of a chaise longue. It may be plain and smooth; shallow buttoned (the buttons are pulled only 13 mm ($\frac{1}{2}$ in) into the fabric, so shallow wrinkles, rather than deep pleats, form around each button); or it may be deep buttoned.

The back section may be lightly padded, as in some dining chairs, or it may be more deeply padded with a stitched roll edge, see p. 112, and finished in one of the ways used for the head rest. The seat is usually plain.

Borders

The seat and all styles of head rest may be finished with a border, which is a separate piece of fabric on the front, applied after the main panel has been attached. The use of a border saves having to pleat the main fabric to reduce fullness around the scroll on the head rest, and often results in a neater finish. Your choice of cover will largely depend on three factors—the original finish (it is often easier to follow this), the type of fabric being used (some patterns and stripes are not suitable for deep buttoning), and the width of the fabric being used (you can often save fabric by cutting separate borders).

Restoring a Chesterfield

A buttoned chesterfield sofa is the aristocrat of living room furniture; and the cost of one reflects its high standing. Why not buy a dilapidated old chesterfield—not necessarily buttoned—strip it down to the bare frame, and re-cover it? For a fraction of the shop price you can own a splendid piece of furniture.

Re-upholstering an item of furniture which would otherwise be on the scrap heap can, in addition, be a satisfying project and lead you on to an absorbing, useful hobby. The techniques detailed here are applicable to all seating that is sprung and stuffed, and will enable you to renovate whole suites of furniture at a fraction of their cost when new or professionally restored.

A buttoned chesterfield has been chosen because it is one of the most difficult projects in upholstery. But while it is not an exercise for the complete novice, it is a feasible proposition if you have had some experience upholstering sofas and chairs. Competence in buttoning and pleating (see p. 118), is important—and so is patience. The professional might take two weeks to do this job; it will take you at least twice as long. Do not try to rush things or invent short cuts.

You will need:
- Mallet with 10cm (4in) head
- Ripping chisel [tack remover], for removing tacks
- 6oz claw or Warrington hammer
- Web strainer or stretcher
- Heavy duty 23cm (9in) scissors
- Curved upholstery needle for springs
- Heavy straight needle 25cm (10in) long for main stitching
- Light straight needle, same length for buttoning
- Small curved needle 75mm (3in) for finishing edge joints
- Regulator or skewer, for regulating stuffing and pleating (see p. 91)

Upholstery materials
The quantity varies with the size of unit being upholstered, but you will need the following:
- Webbing, to anchor the springs
- Springs
- Heavy canvas, about 340g (12oz)
- Light weight canvas or scrim [burlap], about 210g (7½oz)
- Hessian [black cambric]
- Cheap calico [muslin] for cover pattern
- Upholstery fabric

Left: *however battered your chesterfield sofa may be, restored and re-covered it will be good for years.*

- Coconut, or moss fibre for the first stuffing
- Horsehair for the top filling
- Upholstery wadding [padding]
- Upholstery tacks
- 3-ply sisal cord for lashing the springs
- Flax twine for stitching and buttoning
- Buttons, if you are deep buttoning the furniture. These must be covered with matching fabric, professionally or by yourself

Stripping down
Strip the sofa down to the bare wood frame, removing every single tack and scrap of fabric. Do this carefully, using the mallet and ripping chisel [tack remover] to pry out the tacks without damaging the wood. Keep any springs and horsehair in good condition as these can be used again. At this stage some repairs to the frame will be necessary. At the very least, the holes caused by removing the tacks will have to be filled with plastic wood, sanded down after the filler has dried. Any other defects, such as loose joints, must be attended to as well. When all repairs have been made, treat any areas which have been affected by woodworm. This should be left until all other repairs to the frame have been completed, because using woodworm fluid first would affect the bonding power of any adhesives used on the joints. Areas so treated must be left to dry for at least a week, otherwise the fluid may spread on to the fabric.

Fixing the seat springs
Turn the frame upside down and begin to secure the webbing across the bottom of the rails, see p. 88. Start with the webbing strips that run from the back to the front. Tack the strips in place, one at a time, on the rear rail and, using, the strainer or stretcher, strain the webbing over the front rail and tack in position. When these strips have been placed, attach the webbing from side rail to side rail. Before stretching and tacking these long strips, weave them in and out of the front to back strips.

Chesterfield sofa

1. *The stretcher or strainer is used to pull the webbing across the frame. The webbing is then held and tacked in place.*

2. *When the webbing has been tacked and interwoven in place, the springs are stitched on top.*

3. *The springs are compressed and held in place by string knotted along the tops and tacked to the frame.*

4. *When the seat springs are in position, heavy canvas is laid over them and nailed to the frame rails.*

5. *The arm and back springs are fixed in place following the original positions, and lashed in place horizontally.*

6. *Coconut fibre is the usual first stuffing, laid in place and compressed under a light canvas cover.*

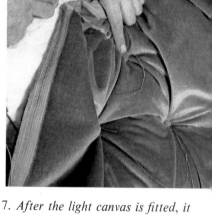

7. *After the light canvas is fitted, it is anchored by stitching through to the heavy canvas below as shown.*

8. *Cut diagonal slits for the buttons and clear holes through the fibre to the base canvas below.*

9. *Horsehair stuffing is placed over the second canvas. Strands of twine hold it in place.*

4

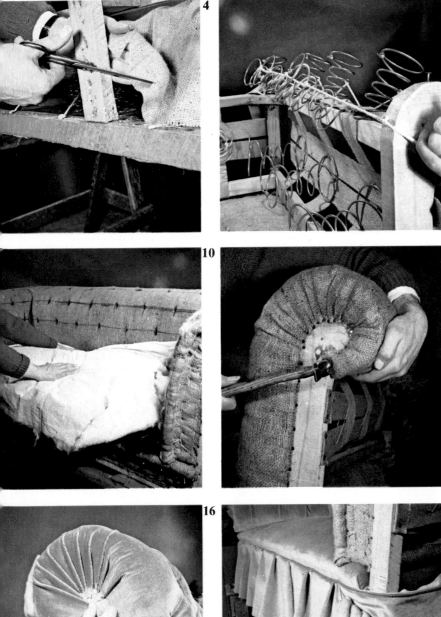

5

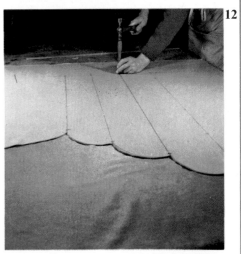

6

10

11

12

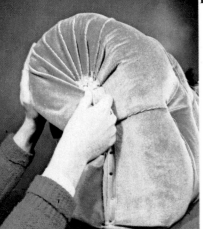

16

17

18

10. *Wadding [padding] is laid over the horsehair and the strands of twine stitched through.*
11. *Be careful when pleating and fitting the front of the arms, it acts as a mould for the final cover.*
12. *Cut out rough patterns in cheap fabric to avoid expensive mistakes.*

13. *Lay the final canvas over the seat and hold it in place with pins while stitching.*
14. *Pull the buttons through. They are secured at the opposite end to the base canvas by a roll of webbing or scrim [burlap].*
15. *Both pleating and buttoning must be done at the same time because of the quantity of loose cover fabric.*

16. *Take care when pleating the cover fabric around the front edges of the arm rest. The nails will be hidden with a separate front panel.*
17. *Fit the skirting panel along the front. After stitching, the fabric is pleated down and nailed under the rail.*
18. *Fit the top seat panel. It is stitched along the front, pleated over to the back and then nailed.*

Then turn the frame right side up and stitch each spring in position (picture 2), using the curved needle, and three stitches, as detailed on p. 105. Lace the tops of the springs down to compress them and hold them in position. To do this, first knot a length of sisal to an outer spring, at a point facing a rail. Take the sisal to the rail and tack it to the rail bottom, then run the sisal across the row of springs to the opposite rail, securing each spring on the way—picture 3 shows a detailed close-up of this process.

As each spring is lashed, compress it about 38 mm (1½ in). Repeat the process across the seat to hold the springs in shape.

Stuffing the seat

Cover the lashed springs with heavy canvas. Fold and tack the canvas along the top of the back rail, then stretch and tack it over the front rail, and finish along the side rails. Stitch the canvas to the tops of the springs in the same way as you stitched the bottoms of the springs to the webbing. Place a 10 cm (4 in)

layer of loose coconut fibre over the seat and cover the filling with light canvas. Stretch the canvas tightly so that it will compress the fibre down to about 38 mm (1½ in). Then tack it down along the back and side rails and stitch it along the front as shown in picture 24—to form a roll. Hold the filling in place by stitching between the two layers of canvas as in picture 7, using the long needle.

Back and side springs

Weave and fix the webbing along

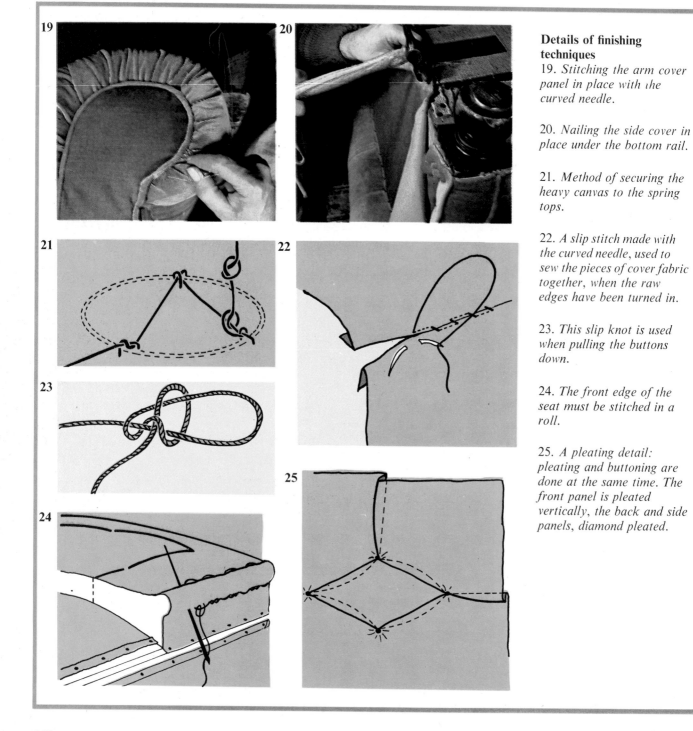

Details of finishing techniques

19. *Stitching the arm cover panel in place with the curved needle.*

20. *Nailing the side cover in place under the bottom rail.*

21. *Method of securing the heavy canvas to the spring tops.*

22. *A slip stitch made with the curved needle, used to sew the pieces of cover fabric together, when the raw edges have been turned in.*

23. *This slip knot is used when pulling the buttons down.*

24. *The front edge of the seat must be stitched in a roll.*

25. *A pleating detail: pleating and buttoning are done at the same time. The front panel is pleated vertically, the back and side panels, diamond pleated.*

the back and arms, tacking and stretching into place in the same way as for the seat. Place the springs in position on the webbing and stitch in place as before. Lash the spring tops as before, but only do so along the length of the sofa, not lengthways and crossways as for the seat. Cover the lashed springs with heavy canvas, stretched and tacked in position, then stitched to the springs.

Back and side fillings
Place a layer of coconut fibre over the back and arms and cover it with light canvas, as for the seat. Then tack the canvas in position along all edges except the arm fronts, tucking the raw edges of the light canvas under. Where the back meets the arms, overlap one edge over the other and turn under the overlapping edge so that the fold lies along the junction of the back and arms. Stitch firmly with a curved needle and twine. For the arm fronts, the fabric is stitched as shown in picture 22 and the filling is tied to the canvases which sandwich the filling.

Button preparation
Mark out the eventual positions of the buttons on the light-weight canvas. With the scissors, cut a diagonal 38 mm (1½ in) slit where each button will be placed. Open up the filling by clearing a hole 30 mm (1¼ in) in diameter through each slit. This is done by inserting the flat end of the regulator or skewer through the slit, and forcing the filling away from the slit all the way down to the first canvas. This will allow the buttons to sink deeply. Mark, slash and clear buttoning holes on seat, back and arms.

The top cover patterns
Ten pieces of fabric will probably be needed for the cover: the front border or panel, seat, inside back, outside back, two inside arms, two outside arms, and two facing panels for the arms. The old cover if carefully removed, may be helpful in cutting new pattern pieces. To work out the dimensions of each piece, measure the length and width

of each area listed above, then add 10 cm (4 in) to each measurement to accommodate the filling and buttoning. Transfer the final dimensions to the cheap calico [muslin] and cut out. These pieces are placed over the final filling to check that the pattern fits, and are then used to outline the cutting for the final covers. Make sure the fabric pattern is accurate, a mistake with the upholstery material can prove expensive.

The final covering
Place 75 mm (3 in) of loose horsehair over the seat area evenly, then lay a layer of wadding [padding] over it. This prevents the horsehair ends from protruding through the cover. You may be able to re-cycle the original horsehair by gentle washing and combing. The wadding [padding] is then tied through the horsehair to the light canvas cover, as in picture 10. Place the fabric seat pattern in position. If the fit is correct, cut the seat cover from the upholstery fabric, making sure the grain is square and, if using a pile fabric, that it runs consistently with the rest of the sofa or you will get an apparent colour change. The seat cover is stitched along the front edge, stretched over the filling, compressing the horsehair to 25 mm (1 in) and tacked in place along the back and sides. The back, arms and front panel are covered with a layer of horsehair and wadding [padding] and the upholstery fabric stretched over in the same way. With these panels you must place and secure the buttons before tacking the edges of the fabric down. The arms must be pleated in ray shaped pleats (picture 16) around the front of the arm rest before being tacked down. The final cover pieces for the back of the seat and arms, the arm fronts and the front panel are stitched and tacked in place.

Any joins to make the required width should be done by the vandyking process described on p. 123, so that the join is hidden in the buttoning. Try to plan joins so that they always come at the junction of the arms with the back. You may

find that you will also have to vandyke a join in the centre of the buttoned back.

Buttoning
To place the buttons, thread a needle and push the eye end of it (use an upholstery needle that is pointed at both ends) through the outside cover and through the shaft in the coconut fibre. When the eye of the needle has just pierced the base canvas, place a 25 mm (1 in) scrap of webbing or canvas between the twine and the needle. This will act as an anchor and prevent the twine from pulling through the canvas. Pull the other end of the needle back through the canvas, out through the main cover, and secure the twine to the button with a slip knot. Pull the twine tight, so that the slip knot forces the button into the filling, but leave the ends loose with a loose end about 10 cm (4 in) long. When all the buttons have been fitted, knot each length of twine, cut the loose ends to about 13 mm (½ in) and tuck under the button (picture 14). As each button is tightened and sunk into position, the fabric must be evenly pleated using the regulator or skewer. The front panel is pleated vertically, the back and side panels are diamond pleated. Start buttoning on the bottom row, working from the centre of each fabric panel to the edges. On the arms, start at the front edge on the bottom row and work towards the back.

When all the buttoning is done, you can attach the front borders, front arm panels and outside panels, turn and stitch the edges to cover raw edges of panels already in place. Finish off the chesterfield with a piece of hessian [black cambric] tacked to the underside of the frame to cover all raw edges and tacks.

Foam rubber can be substituted for the second layer of stuffing—the horsehair and wadding [padding]. You may find it easier to work with and to get an even effect with, than the traditional methods. You can mark a buttoning pattern on the surface of the foam, as a guide.

Living with Your Beautiful Bargains

You will be lucky indeed if your beautiful bargains include pieces from the great age of furniture—1720-1820. Most of them are in museums and the most luxurious of homes. Do not envy them; it seems that, since antiques became big business, many prized pieces are fakes—even museums have been hoaxed. So instead of an expensive piece with barely a genuine leg to stand on, look for the items you can afford. Look for oak furniture, solid, childproof, whether genuinely old or repro; look for bentwood, first of the great mass-produced furniture, decorative, strong, light; look for Victorian pieces, no longer going for the song they used to, but usually well made and often highly decorative; look for Edwardian pieces, which are often bargain-priced because they are much too big for today's homes, but which can be divided up; look for solid articles from between World War I and World War II, stripped of their gravy-coloured varnish they get a whole new look; look for plain whitewood and take time to give it the individual touch it needs. Do not dismiss a piece as it stands: cultivate an eye for possibilities.

A dozen ideas for your home

1. Your furniture is basically modern—you have a modern square-lined suite. Add a touch of visual interest with smaller period pieces. Look, for example, for a period mantelpiece (negotiate with the foreman of a demolition site); try a small period table or two, an old chest for a coffee table, an odd old chair, re-upholstered, perhaps in a modern fabric. It can add visual interest to a run of the mill room.

2. Make a period sofa the star of the room if everything else is starkly modern. A chesterfield sofa looks good anywhere, with any style of furnishing. Use a substantial modern upholstery fabric instead of the usual classic velvet.

3. If your room has a traditional look, give it all a fresh look with an up-to-date colour scheme instead of

play-safe Regency stripes or subdued colours which everyone thinks are correct. Use modern patterns, fresh colours, novel textures when re-upholstering your finds.

4. You like your furniture traditional, your woods wood-like, your carpets classic? Why not pick a fashion colour from a prevailing pattern and put it on your walls. Modern, quick-drying emulsion paints make the job a weekend one.

Choose a matching gloss for your woodwork, it makes the subtlest tone-on-tone colour touch.

5. If you like the 'cottagey' look —it is especially comforting to town dwellers—buy your bargains and strip them all back to the wood, then give them a clear finish.

Below: *some old, sturdy, reproduction furniture and a modern patterned floor covering go well together in today's dining rooms.*

Let all the different wood tones mingle for visual interest. Strip your doors, floors and woodwork too, if you have the energy and patience. A 'no-colour' room can be very restful.

6. Use white as a background for your beautiful bargains—white floor (Flokati [white throw] rugs which are washable), white walls, white modern storage furniture. Modern white paints stay white longer, modern smokeless zone environments keep things cleaner. There is nothing like white (and there are many shades of white on the paint card, from warm to cool) for showing off the shapes of furniture.

7. Liven up a 'safe' room with a fantasy piece. This could be a plain piece of furniture given a decorative finish, or a complicated shape painted a stunning colour. It could be small like a coffee table, an eye-catcher like a curlicued Victorian sideboard, a whitewood chest, or possibly an odd-looking chair. Just let yourself go in one area.

8. Buy a set of non-matching bargain chairs and paint them all to match your bargain dining table. Black is still the most sophisticated, understated colour, or you could go for the most fashion-conscious new shade being marketed. Paint is a wonderful way to disguise re-conditioned surfaces and pull a

roomful of mis-matches together.

9. Buy a plain piece of unfinished furniture and make it fit in with your precious period pieces by painstakingly giving it everything a period piece needs—new hardware, a grained realistic finish, mouldings and so on. Get the ideas from a book, a museum or a stately home. Dent or scratch it a bit, too, to give it that heirloom look.

10. Conversely, buy an unattractive old piece and streamline it—cut

Below: *a scrubbed pine table and non-matching chairs.* Opposite: *traditional 'stick-back' chairs help to enliven and humanize an ultra-efficient modern kitchen.*

down the legs, perhaps, take off the fancy bits, change the hardware, give it a teak or rosewood grain finish, or a sleek matt paint job.

11. Do not in your passion for the all-period look, try to find things that did not exist, like period hi-fi cabinets, coffee tables, standard lamps and so on. Modern lighting, modern comfortable sofas and chairs, modern small tables—all in classic modern shapes will look better. You can always cover or paint them to go with your scheme. Our forbears did not lounge as we do—many period pieces just do not feel comfortable to modern bodies.

12. If you find a real period piece, restore and re-finish it carefully. You could live with it for a while and then sell it, probably for more than you paid. Then, buy something that bit better—this is often called 'trading up' and it is one way to even more beautiful bargains!

Below: a good example of a stunning piece of furniture, which would highlight a modern or traditional room.

Glossary

Acrylic paint: emulsion, water-based paints, of various acrylic esters and other polymers.

Alkyd resin: basic chemical ingredients of many paints and finishes.

Animal glue: traditional adhesive made from the natural gelatine in skins and bones.

Back-tacking: a method of joining two parts of a furniture covering so that the stitches do not show.

Batten: a narrow length of wood.

Beading: a narrow wood moulding used as a decorative finish to a piece of furniture.

Bevel: The slanting edge of a chisel or surface.

Bit: the part of a hand or power drill which makes the screw hole or withdraws the screw.

Blockboard: a man-made board consisting of a thin veneer of wood top and bottom with a core of other wood.

Bowing: warping in wood which results in a bend along the entire grain of the piece.

Bradawl: a carpentry tool used for making small holes in wood.

Bridle ties: special stitches used to hold upholstery stuffing in place.

Carborundum: particles of this material are used to make oilstones which help give a fine edge to cutting tools such as chisels.

Carcass: the basic frame of a piece of furniture.

Chamfer: giving an angled surface to a wood edge so that tacks or nails may be driven into it.

Chipboard: man-made board made from compressed wood particles.

Chisel: sharp edged tool used for shaping wood.

Clamp: versatile device used for holding pieces of wood together.

Claw hammer: hammer with pronged head useful for extracting nails.

Crosshead screw: modern design screw with cross-shaped slot in the head which gives the correct screwdriver a better grip.

Cabinet scraper

Crowbar: a strong piece of metal used for levering.

Dowel, dowel rod: a slender rod-shaped piece of turned wood.

Ebonizing: a wood finish imitating ebony.

Epoxy resin adhesive: modern formula adhesive used for heavy-duty work.

Filing: shaping a piece of wood or metal with the appropriate filing tool.

Fill: prepare a smooth surface with wood or other filler.

Fillet: a narrow piece of wood.

Flour-grade paper: a fine grade of sandpaper used for the most delicate stages of furniture finishing.

French chalk: white powder used for absorbing and marking-out processes.

French polish: a mixture of shellac and methylated spirits [denatured alcohol] used to give a clear, traditional finish to wood furniture.

Fronds: leaf of a palm or fern.

Gimlet: a carpentry tool used for making small holes in wood.

Grain: the natural marking and texture of wood.

Grain filling: a stage in the building up of a fine finish on furniture which fills the natural indentations of a particular wood grain to give a smoother surface.

Graphite: a natural lubricant.

Hardboard: a thin sheet material made from compressed pulped softwood.

Hardware: metal attachments like knobs, hinges, locks etc., applied to a piece of furniture.

Inlay: pieces of one wood or other material, inserted in a decorative pattern.

Key: to prepare a surface by roughening for painting or finishing.

Knot: a natural irregularity (usually round or oval) in wood which must be sealed before a perfect finish is possible.

Knotting: special shellac preparation used for sealing knots in wood.

Laminate: a modern material made of compressed resin impregnated paper, generally applied as a finishing veneer to a base material.

Latex: natural rubber.

Lath: a thin, narrow length of wood.

Marquetry: work inlaid with pieces of various-coloured wood.

Matt: a dull, not glossy surface.

Member: part of a piece of furniture or furniture frame.

Moss fibre: a stuffing material used in upholstery.

Nail punch [punch or nail set]:

carpentry tool used for driving the nail head below a wood surface.

Oil paint: paint which uses oil as its medium – as opposed to a water-based paint.

Over-stuffed: upholstery which is built up to curve over the edge of a piece of furniture.

Panel pin [finishing nail]: a fine nail with small head used for cabinet work.

Panel saw: used for ripping (cutting down the wood grain) and cross-cutting (cutting across the grain).

Patina: a gleaming surface on furniture produced by years of dusting and polishing.

Planing: smoothing and shaping wood with a plane.

Polyurethane: a modern synthetic resin used in modern paints and finishes.

Primer: the basic coat applied to raw wood to seal the surface.

Pva adhesive: polyvinyl acetate adhesive used for woodworking.

Pva: polyvinyl acetate – a polymerised derivative of ethylene (a colourless gas) used as a base for modern adhesives, paints etc.

Rail: horizontal members in a chair, table or other furniture frame.

Rottenstone: a natural abrasive material used in furniture finishing.

Regulator: a special upholstery tool used for making deep buttoned pleats and to adjust stuffing materials.

Sand: to smooth wood or a wood finish with abrasive paper or steel wool.

Screw sink bit: a drill attachment used to make a screw hole which is shaped so that the head of the screw can be driven below the wood surface.

Scriber: carpentry tool used to mark wood.

Selvedge [selvage]: the edge of a piece of fabric where it is tightly woven to prevent fraying.

Shavehook: a tool specially shaped for scraping paint or finish from corners and mouldings.

Shavehook [paint scraper]

Splat: the vertical centre piece of wood in a chair back.

Shellac: a natural resin used traditionally for varied wood finishing processes.

Slip stitching: a method of stitching one piece of an upholstery cover to another.

Steel wool: abrasive material used in varied degrees of coarseness for wood finishing.

Stretcher: the part of a chair frame which runs horizontally from side to side under a chair seat to hold the legs apart.

Stripper, stripping: the use of chemical or mechanical ways to remove paint or finish from a wood surface.

Tack bar: a separate piece of wood above the back rail of a chair seat used for attaching the covering fabric.

Tease: to loosen compressed fibres.

Temporary-tack: a tack placed half-way in for later removal, or finally to be driven home.

Tenon or back saw: a saw with a stiffened back which helps achieve a straight cut in fine woodwork.

Thermoplastic: material which can be softened and shaped when heated.

Thixotropic: a property of many modern paints which gives a jelly-like consistency.

Tongue and groove joint: a basic carpentry joint in which the projection on one piece fits into a groove in another.

Tourniquet: an improvised sling used to hold parts of a piece of furniture together while the adhesive dries.

Trimming knife: multi-purpose handyman's knife often with a selection of blades for different materials.

Undercoat: the coat or coats of paint used over the primer and under the finishing coat.

Veneer: a thin piece of decorative or precious wood applied to a stable base or wood core.

Veneer pin: extra fine nail used for attaching mouldings to furniture.

Vice [vise]: clamping device used to hold wood firmly in place on a working bench.

Warp: distortion of a piece of wood through heat or damp.

Welt: a piece of fabric in a chair or sofa cover or cushion which accommodates the thickness of the particular part of the piece.

Wet and dry paper: a waterproof sandpaper used for preparing surfaces for paint or finish. Water is used as a lubricant.

Whitespirit [mineralspirits]: petroleum distillate used as a substitute for natural turpentine.

Wood filler: a preparation which becomes hard when dry and which is used to level holes or irregularities in a wood surface.

Index

An American supplier of general
tools is detailed below. Two British
suppliers – one of upholstery
materials and tools and another of
carpentry tools are also listed.

(*general tools*)
Woodcraft Supply Corp.
313 Montvale Avenue,
Woburn, Mass. 01801.

(*upholstery materials and tools*)
Russell Trading Co.,
75 Paradise Street,
Liverpool.
(mail order catalogue available)

(*carpentry tools*)
Buck and Ryan,
101 Tottenham Court Road,
London W.1.